Thank you for your
leadership in Seattle and throughout
our nation.
With gratitude,

— Kent

PLACE-BASED COMMUNITY ENGAGEMENT
IN HIGHER EDUCATION

Connie,
Thank you for your interest
in the book and support.

Emma K. Y

PLACE-BASED COMMUNITY ENGAGEMENT IN HIGHER EDUCATION

A Strategy to Transform Universities and Communities

Erica K. Yamamura and Kent Koth

Foreword by Geoffrey Canada

STERLING, VIRGINIA

Library of Congress Cataloging-in-Publication Data
Names: Yamamura, Erica K., 1978- author. |
Koth, Kent, 1967- author.
Title: Place-based community engagement in higher education : a
strategy to transform universities and communities /
Erica K. Yamamura and Kent Koth ; foreword by Geoffrey Canada.
Description: First edition. |
Sterling, Virginia : Stylus Publishing, 2018. |
Includes bibliographical references and index. |
Identifiers: LCCN 2017044373 (print) |
LCCN 2017061537 (ebook) |
ISBN 9781620366783 (Library networkable e-edition) |
ISBN 9781620366790 (Consumer e-edition) |
ISBN 9781620366776 (pbk. : alk. paper) |
ISBN 9781620366769 (cloth : alk. paper)
Subjects: LCSH: Community and college--United States. |
Education, Higher--Social aspects--United States. |
Universities and colleges--United States--Public services.
Classification: LCC LC238 (ebook) | LCC LC238 .Y36 2018 (print) |
DDC 378.1/03--dc23
LC record available at https://lccn.loc.gov/2017044373

13-digit ISBN: 978-1-62036-676-9 (cloth)
13-digit ISBN: 978-1-62036-677-6 (paperback)
13-digit ISBN: 978-1-62036-678-3 (library networkable e-edition)
13-digit ISBN: 978-1-62036-679-0 (consumer e-edition)

Printed in the United States of America

All first editions printed on acid-free paper
that meets the American National Standards Institute

Z39-48 Standard.

Bulk Purchases
Quantity discounts are available for use in workshops
and for staff development.
Call 1-800-232-0223

First Edition, 2018

CONTENTS

FOREWORD

In the 1990s, my staff and I began planning the Harlem Children's Zone Project to tackle all the problems our kids and community faced: violence, drugs, bad schools, terrible health care, and homelessness. It seemed like a bold if not crazy thing to do, since no one had ever attempted to do this for low-income kids on such a large scale. But we needed to do something big enough to address the massive crisis we were facing in Harlem, in New York City, and across the United States.

Today, the Harlem Children's Zone serves more than 12,500 children and can point to transformational change for an entire neighborhood. Our goal was to break the cycle of generational poverty through education, and now more than 90% of our high-school seniors are routinely accepted to college. Nine hundred students are sitting in college classrooms, not on park benches or in prison cells. Success is becoming the norm just as it is in middle-class communities. It was not magic. We created a solid business plan for a birth-through-college pipeline of services and worked hard and long to execute that plan.

While our focus was to help our children in Harlem, we also hoped that our work would lead the way for other communities to save their children with similar comprehensive plans. In 2003, we created the Practitioners Institute, a group that would provide consistent guidance to communities about what we do and how we got there. We have had hundreds of communities take our workshops so they could take some sure first steps toward creating their own projects.

Certainly the need is there. The United States has 14.5 million children stuck in grinding poverty within a country that is the richest in history. I believe our country has the resources and rationale to break the cycle of generational poverty for many more children. What we did in Harlem can be replicated—and universities can play a key role in making that happen.

While these initiatives must be based in the community itself, universities can provide some of the intellectual capital that impoverished communities often lack. These community-based efforts have to encompass "street smarts" and "book smarts" working together, united in the common purpose of educating children. Even a great plan in writing will fail if the community is not respected and treated as a valuable, equal partner. Poor people are rightfully suspicious when someone from outside the community suddenly arrives and tells them that they, their parents, and their grandparents have been living their lives wrong. That said, universities can bring to bear state-of-the-art research on best practices regarding brain development, education, and health.

An important step for which universities are well-suited is creating a business plan for transforming a community. If done properly, a business plan can serve as a road map that guides how the process will unfold over the years, including specific goals, milestones, and markers. Getting a child successfully through college is a 20-year project, and, for an organization, it is critical that a solid set of goals is present to flag any stumble and allow staff and families to track each child.

The institutional heft of universities can bring other critical resources to a fledgling project addressing a devastated community. Universities can provide an important base for administrative support, which is necessary to hold together often overlooked functions such as hiring, record-keeping, accounting, and managing payroll. Universities can also provide assurances to large funders, such as foundations and corporations, who may be hesitant about giving to an initiative that has little or no track record.

Solving the problem of generational poverty should be the nation's universities' top priority. Their partnership can strengthen our country and provide a real-world laboratory and incredible learning experience for their staff and students. I am certain that many would be inspired by the wisdom and heroism they will find in these struggling, forgotten communities.

Visionary leaders in the academic community know their students and faculty cannot thrive by living walled off from the world around them. I urge all of our universities to step forward and engage in the work to create a rising tide of opportunity for all of America's children.

The arrival of *Place-Based Community Engagement in Higher Education: A Strategy to Transform Universities and Communities* is particularly welcome because it provides universities with both the theory and practical logistics for pursuing community-based work. This book invites universities to pursue deeper and more powerful partnerships with the communities around them, helping to create a comprehensive strategy for changing the odds of disadvantaged children as we have done in Harlem.

Geoffrey Canada
President, Harlem Children's Zone

Over the past several decades, universities across the nation have significantly increased their commitment to engaging their campuses in their communities. Utilizing service-learning, community-based research, student-led projects, and other forms of community engagement, these institutions have mobilized thousands of students and faculty to partner with local organizations, schools, and institutions. All too often, these efforts have focused much more on college student learning than on impact in the wider community. In addition, even when taking community outcomes more seriously, many universities lack a coordinated and strategic focus, therefore limiting their ability to maximize their impact in the larger community.

The emerging model of place-based community engagement offers universities a powerful tool to attain more positive results in their local communities and also on their campuses. Perhaps most widely known through the work of the Harlem Children's Zone and the federal government's Promise and Choice Neighborhoods programs, place-based initiatives focus on uniting disparate leaders, services, and institutions to positively address the often intractable challenge of geographically concentrated poverty and other contemporary issues of inequity and injustice. Drawing upon the concept of collective impact and using data-driven decision-making, place-based initiatives build long-term partnerships based upon a shared vision. When done thoughtfully, these place-based initiatives have attained impressive results.

While offering immense benefits, place-based community engagement also brings new challenges. A more pronounced commitment to community impact can compel the university to engage its community as equitable stakeholders. Place-based community engagement also raises resource and funding issues as the approach often calls for additional investments in staff, faculty, and partners. Finally, place-based community engagement often means bridging historically White universities with diverse cultural and racial communities, raising many additional questions regarding power, privilege, and community voice.

Through this book we explore how universities can utilize a place-based community engagement model to significantly deepen and expand their impact on campus and in the community. Drawing on lessons learned from five institutions that have implemented place-based community engagement initiatives, we examine the opportunities, challenges, and considerations for universities hoping to pursue a place-based approach. By sharing practices from these five institutions, we provide a detailed process of taking a place-based effort from exploration to sustainability in order to attain results beyond what any one department, organization, or institution thought possible.

We believe that place-based community engagement offers institutions of higher education a powerful tool to become more connected to their communities, with a goal of transforming their campuses, their local communities, and our nation.

How Did This Book Come About?

In 2011, after a multiyear planning process, Seattle University launched the Seattle University Youth Initiative, an intensive university-wide effort to empower and support children and families within a neighborhood encompassing 100 square blocks adjacent to the university campus. As the Youth Initiative experienced success, delegations from other universities visited Seattle to learn about the initiative. In 2014, the Annie E. Casey Foundation provided support to Seattle University to convene teams from other institutions in order to share ideas and strategies to pursue place-based community engagement. In the ensuing years, the Annie E. Casey Foundation and Seattle University have continued to partner on offering several additional institutes on place-based community engagement and other forms of professional development. Through this work, together they have begun to develop a national network of universities, particularly faith-based institutions, interested in place-based community engagement.

In tandem with the institutes, we collaborated on writing two white papers that summarized lessons learned from Seattle University's intensive place-based efforts. We also shared lessons and ideas through workshops and keynote addresses at several regional and national convenings and professional conferences. In an effort to capitalize on the interest in this work and provide a wider perspective than just Seattle University, we began to explore a book project. Our idea of writing a book became a reality when Erica K. Yamamura received support to work on the endeavor as her sabbatical project.

This was truly a collaborative project by two professionals who, taken together, view this project through an intersectional practitioner-scholar worldview. Kent Koth draws first from the strong practitioner lens that he has developed over the last 25 years of facilitating campus and community initiatives at several institutions of higher education. In working on this project, Koth drew upon insights into the political, social, and psychological dynamics internal and external to a university community engagement office. He also brought to the project his experiences of planning and implementing the Seattle University Youth Initiative. Koth's motivation for this project arose from a lifelong belief that we are so much stronger working together than operating in isolation.

Throughout this project Yamamura leaned on her strong research lens as a faculty member, drawing upon her training at the University of California, Los Angeles (UCLA) Higher Education Research Institute where she served as a graduate research assistant on the Atlantic Philanthropies research project, which examined the benefits of service-learning in the years following graduation. She served as the methodologist for the book and took the lead with our Institutional Research Board (IRB, which identified this work as IRB exempt), working on document acquisition and analysis, coding and analysis of data, development of findings, and the member-checking process. Yamamura also drew upon her analytical and theoretical understanding of institutions of higher education, organizational development, and her explorations of race, class, and privilege. Yamamura is not new to the field of service-learning and community engagement. She participated in many opportunities through the UCLA Asian American Studies Center as an undergraduate student, and later as a graduate student she coordinated educational internships, AmeriCorps and Bonner Foundation fellowships, and K–12 partnerships at the UCLA Center for Community Learning. Yamamura's motivation for this project is to give back to the field of service-learning and community engagement and help it move forward in a meaningful way.

Our unique strengths led us to have many robust conversations about what institutions to study; what constitutes strong analysis; what would be most pertinent to scholars and practitioners; and, ultimately, what would lead to a compelling book that contributes to a more just and compassionate society.

The Organization of This Book

Universities and communities that want to pursue place-based community engagement can improve their likelihood of success by carefully studying their specific contexts and assessing their opportunities and potential challenges. This book is designed to offer a framework for how to plan for and pursue a place-based community engagement strategy.

Chapter 1 examines several dynamics that are significantly challenging contemporary higher education and also presents the evolving paradigm of community engagement within higher education. We draw upon these explorations to frame the potential benefits of pursuing a place-based community engagement strategy.

Chapter 2 provides an overview of the existing landscape of place-based community engagement across the United States. The chapter also defines key tenets of place-based community engagement, especially how this unique approach draws on numerous roles of the university to connect to a geographic sense of place. We close the chapter by introducing three distinct phases for effective place-based community engagement.

Chapter 3 presents the methodology of our research that guided the structure and development of this book. We also introduce five institutional case studies that we draw upon in subsequent chapters: Drexel University, Loyola University Maryland, San Diego State University, Seattle University, and the University of San Diego.

Chapters 4 to 6 draw upon specific examples and trends arising from the five institutional case studies to offer practical guidance for putting concepts into action. We organize these chapters based on the three distinct phases of place-based community engagement: (a) exploration, (b) development, and (c) sustaining. Taken together, these phases frame many of the opportunities and challenges involved in place-based community engagement.

In chapter 7 we again draw from the institutional case studies to highlight the vantage point of community leaders who have chosen to partner with universities to pursue place-based community engagement. From the perspective of community partners, we examine what has worked, what has been challenging, and overall lessons arising from place-based community engagement.

Chapter 8 explores strategies and promising practices with assessment and outcomes throughout the various phases of place-based community engagement. In addition, we also explore approaches to share and disseminate data and results.

Finally, in chapter 9 we draw upon our definition of *place-based community engagement* to summarize the lessons and challenges arising from the place-based approach. We also highlight numerous questions that remain to be answered and explored.

This book is not meant to be a blueprint but rather to present ideas, practices, and lessons to draw upon in exploring, developing, and sustaining a place-based community engagement strategy. There is not one model of place-based community engagement. Institutions and their respective communities operate in differing contexts and have different opportunities and challenges. We offer this book as an invitation to explore concepts and methods that could lead to transformation of individual institutions and communities and also foster renewal and innovation in the field of higher education as a whole.

ACKNOWLEDGMENTS

First and foremost, we are thankful to all of the community organizations and community members who shared their experiences with us as partners of the universities we examined in this book. Without your partnership and support in reimagining community engagement, this book would not be possible.

We are thankful to Seattle University for providing the time and resources to complete this project. We particularly thank Stephen Sundborg, S.J., and Jim Sinegal for their steadfast belief in the power of Seattle University and its community partners working together to pursue transformative change. We also wish to thank current and past leaders at Seattle University, including Isiaah Crawford, Jacob Diaz, Robert Dullea, Robert Kelly, Michele Murray, Joe Orlando, Deanna Sands, and Alvin Sturdivant. We are extremely grateful for the insights and support of our colleagues in the College of Education Student Development Administration program and the staff, students, and supporters of the Center for Community Engagement; you enrich our lives.

We have so much gratitude for our colleagues at Drexel University, Loyola University Maryland, San Diego State University, and the University of San Diego, including Mindy Hohman, Jennifer Kebea, Lucy Kerman, Chris Nayve, Erin O'Keefe, and Stephen Weber. We appreciated your hospitality during our visits and your openness to sharing your wisdom with us. You all are an inspiration. Thank you to Robert Price and Rosario Martinez Iannacone from Price Philanthropies for sharing your many insights from your work in City Heights. Special thanks to our mentors and colleagues in the field of community engaged research and practice for inspiring our work and for your support over the years: Jeffrey Anderson, Sefa Aina, Jim Burklo, Mitch Chang, Nadinne Cruz, Chuck Dorn, Yarrow Durbin, Miguel Guajardo, Don Hill, Jennifer Huntington, Ron Krabill, Jennifer Obidah, Kathy O'Byrne, Debra Pounds, Cesie Delve Scheuermann, Jackie Schmidt Posner, and Lori Vogelgesang.

Marshall Welch, thank you for reviewing and discussing our early prospectus and for offering numerous invaluable insights. John von Knorring, thank you for your interest in this topic, for your belief in us as a team, and for your long commitment to amplifying compelling ideas that are transforming higher education. McKenzie Baker and Robert Duggan, we appreciate your support in editing and graphic design. Thank you to Charles Rutheiser of the Annie E. Casey Foundation; your national perspective pushed us to think more expansively. Geoffrey Canada, it is your vision and inspiration that we draw upon in connecting our university and our neighborhoods; you are truly an American hero.

We are thankful for our first teachers, our parents. Erica thanks her parents, Kyoko and Yukito Yamamura, for instilling in her the love of reading that led her to becoming a professor and now a book author. She also thanks Lene and Kjeld Nielsen, Tomas Hannibal Nielsen, and Hanne Rasmussen, for their encouragement and support. Kent thanks his mom, Anne; as an English teacher you influenced his love of writing. Kent also thanks his father, Gene; while you have left us, your teachings live on in him and in so many others. Kent also thanks Diana Yeh and John, Sheri, and Taylor Koth for their support and inspiration.

Projects like this one often mean long hours of solitary reading and writing and site visits that take one away from home. And frequently, this means that laundry does not get done, dishes remain unwashed, and children wonder where their parents have gone. Thank you to our families for your patience, care, and love throughout this project and throughout our lives. Soren, Malia, Ling, Nadiya, and Kalani—we love you and we thank you.

PART ONE

INTRODUCTION, CONTEXT, AND METHODOLOGY

INTRODUCTION TO PLACE-BASED COMMUNITY ENGAGEMENT

Contemporary higher education is facing significant challenges and uncertainty. At the same time, our wider society is in a period of significant upheaval, with a breakdown in civil discourse and a growing gap between competing political and philosophical beliefs. Perhaps more than ever universities and communities need each other to address the challenges they face. Unfortunately, although traditional approaches to community engagement in higher education have many strong merits, they are not fully capable of responding to these changing times.

All too frequently, contemporary community engagement efforts in higher education focus more on student learning and faculty research over pursuing measurable change on larger societal issues. With this tendency to face inward, most universities are not fully utilizing their ability to be agents of change in their local communities. To respond to our present moment, university and community leaders must develop new ways of partnering that place greater emphasis on mutual benefit. Place-based community engagement provides a powerful way to creatively connect campus and community to foster positive social transformation.

This chapter highlights a few of the emerging trends and challenges facing higher education and also briefly describes the historical and current context of community engagement in higher education. Next, we introduce and discuss the benefits of pursuing place-based community engagement and how this approach differs from traditional service-learning as well as the anchor institution paradigm.

Current Higher Education Context

Responding to the shifting political and economic climate, higher education today is in the midst of organizational change. For families, the rising cost of a college education is an ongoing challenge—on average, private tuition at U.S. colleges is $37,990, and public tuition is $18,632 (U.S. Department of Education National Center for Education Statistics, 2016). The decline in public student aid is yet another challenge that students and their families, especially low-income families, must overcome to participate in higher education (Goldrick-Rab, 2016; Kelly, Howell, & Sattin-Bajaj, 2016). For universities across the country, the increase in federal oversight and compliance; the need to update aging facilities; and the desire to differentiate through innovative and often costly events, facilities, and opportunities have contributed to an increase in administrators and staff, further adding to the cost of education.

Financial Challenges

For public institutions, the continued decline in state funding raises a significant financial challenge. To address these financial pressures, many universities are turning to a business model of education, one that focuses on inputs such as student enrollment and strives for a clearer financial return on investment (Craig, 2015; Selingo, 2013). Community colleges in multiple states are offering baccalaureate degrees, which helps these institutions generate revenue yet becomes an added financial pressure for traditional four-year institutions (Bailey, Jaggars, & Jenkins, 2015). The need to generate new forms of revenue is especially omnipresent at tuition-dependent institutions, in particular those that are less selective and have more modest endowments.

To increase revenue and diversity on their campuses, many institutions are increasing their international student recruitment and admissions. Many public institutions have also sought to increase the percentage of out-of-state students, as these students typically are charged higher tuition than in-state students (Lewin, 2012). Yet, on occasion, state legislators have pushed back and in some cases passed legislation to limit the percentage of out-of-state students attending state institutions, such as with the University of California (Watanabe, 2017).

Diversity in Higher Education

The effort to reach and better help underserved students is yet another important part of the changing context of higher education (Museus & Jayakumar, 2012; Pérez & Ceja, 2015). Responding to the needs of undocumented students, a growing number of colleges are offering specialized programs and advising to this student population (Perez, 2009). Veterans' programs and services is another area of growth (Karp & Klempin, 2016; Steele, Saucedo, & Coley, 2010). Many campuses have developed specific programs to respond to the unique needs of transfer students, who tend to be older and are more likely to have children and families than traditional first-time full-time freshmen (Karp & Klempin, 2016). Finally, Men of Color initiatives have also grown to enhance retention of this student population (Knight & Marciano, 2013; Sáenz, Ponjuán, & López Figueroa, 2016).

Expanding Modalities: Online, Hybrid, and Global Campuses

Another shift within higher education is the expansion of modalities of learning environments (Craig, 2015; Crow & Dabars, 2015; Selingo, 2013). The rise of massive open online courses (MOOCs) and cost-free online outlets such as the Khan Academy have opened up higher education to more individuals. Responding to these phenomena, most colleges today offer online courses which may be asynchronous (do not meet at a regular time), hybrid (some combination of online and in-person), or synchronous (meet online at a regular time). Some institutions have created entire degrees that do not require a student to ever be present on the physical campus. Although this modality has been popular with graduate programs for some time, recently there has been a surge of undergraduate programs that are also moving in this direction. The Colorado State University-Global Campus and online degree completion programs for students who are military veterans are two examples of this growing trend.

Activism

Activism among college students is not new. From the protests for ethnic studies in California in the 1960s to advocacy for affirmative action in the 1980s, there is a long history of activism on college campuses (Park, 2013). Yet recently, as campuses have become more diverse and students have faced increasing financial burdens, there has been a rise of student activism focused on making campuses more inclusive (Muñoz, 2015; Perez, 2009). For example, protests led by undocumented students and their allies eventually led some states to change in-state tuition policies to include undocumented students.

More recently, student-led campus protests arising from the Black Lives Matter movement have pushed universities to reexamine practices and policies to better address campus issues related to race and racism. On our own campus, students protested historical and present racism in the curriculum and among faculty (Ramsey, Bono, Lin, & Turner, 2016). Largely as a result of these protests, university leaders moved quickly to address students' concerns and created a new position of chief diversity officer.

The challenges we describe have led some to question the value and relevance of higher education in today's society. Universities must respond to this concern in a thoughtful and intentional manner by continuing to focus on their mission and values while seeking new approaches to contributing to their wider communities. Place-based community engagement, which connects campus and community in multilayered ways, may be one of the additional methods universities can utilize to respond to contemporary challenges and demonstrate their critical importance to society.

Current Landscape of Community Engagement in Higher Education

Over the past four decades, a community engagement movement has arisen on college and university campuses across the United States as well as in other countries. Fueled by a desire to better educate students while positively contributing to communities, universities have developed community engagement offices, advocated for the development of service-learning courses, and encouraged students to volunteer with local and international organizations. Far from static, the field of community engagement in higher education has evolved significantly since its early origins (Post, Ward, Longo, & Saltmarsh, 2016).

In the 1980s college students on campuses throughout the United States began volunteering at local organizations and self-organizing efforts to address local issues. In recognition of this trend and also in response to the critique that college students were self-obsessed and materialistic—a part of the "me generation"—in 1985 three college presidents founded Campus Compact, inviting other presidents to join a coalition to promote civic engagement on their campuses (Hartley & Saltmarsh, 2016). At about the same time, several recent college graduates formed the Campus Outreach Opportunity League (COOL) to provide students with a platform to engage with each other in order to develop leadership skills for serving and learning in communities (Hartley & Saltmarsh, 2016).

Building upon student interest and the nascent national organizing efforts, in the 1990s and early 2000s, faculty began to integrate service into university curricula as service-learning became more formalized and widespread. Campus Compact (Heffernan, 2001), the American Association for Higher Education's 21-book series (e.g., Erickson & Anderson, 1997; Hardin, Eribes, & Poster, 2006; Ward, 1999), and many other organizations and scholars began to develop publications to assist faculty in deepening their practice of service-learning in the university classroom and community. During this period, many universities also formed centers for service and service-learning, and hundreds of institutions became members of Campus Compact (Hartley & Saltmarsh, 2016).

As service-learning gained popularity and became institutionalized, research began to show the impact of service-learning participation on college students (Astin, Vogelgesang, Ikeda, & Yee, 2000; Eyler & Giles, 1999). At about the same time, scholars developed rubrics to assess the level of institutionalization of service-learning and community engagement (Furco, 1999; Holland, 1997). Responding to the need to justify investments in community engagement, much of the subsequent research has also focused on student and faculty experiences with service-learning.

In 2006, the Carnegie Foundation created a Community Engagement classification, inviting institutions of higher education to apply for this designation. Since 2006, three additional classification processes have occurred (2008, 2010, and 2015), and scholars have reviewed successful applications to develop strategies and tools to help institutions further advance their efforts (Welch, 2016). The classification places a heavy emphasis on university institutional systems and processes, with relatively limited focus on community impact.

Over the past 20 years the field of community engagement has become more nuanced, refined, and self-critical. The concept of mutuality in service and service-learning has emerged (Rhoads, 1997), and substantial critiques of service-learning have also arisen (Butin, 2006; Mitchell, 2008). Scholars and national leaders have also advocated for a better understanding of service-learning across cultures and races (Mitchell, Donahue, & Young-Law, 2012; Stewart & Webster, 2011) and the use of asset-based frameworks over more traditional deficit or problem-based paradigms (Plaut & Hamerlinck, 2014). A few scholars and practitioners have also begun to shift from the focus on student learning toward greater emphasis on long-term partnerships with community organizations and more significant community impact (Guajardo, Guajardo, Janson, & Militello, 2016; Stoecker, 2016; Stoecker & Tryon, 2009).

One additional emerging community engagement strategy is the anchor institution concept that calls upon universities to expansively leverage their resources to better address the needs of their urban communities (Hodges & Dubb, 2012). An anchor institution strategy extends beyond academic service-learning and student volunteerism. As Hodges and Dubb (2012) highlight, "it is a strategic re-orientation of a university mission to focus its resources [academic and non-academic] . . . to assist in community economic development and local problem-solving work" (p. xx). The anchor strategy could extend into nearly every aspect of the university: from purchasing to hiring, from housing to economic development. Although promising, this approach also has limits as it frequently depends on a presidential mandate with strong buy-in from the targeted communities.

As community engagement in higher education continues to mature and evolve, additional approaches and strategies are needed to build upon the successes and limitations of the programs and models that have been developed over the past four decades. For many institutions of higher education, place-based community engagement may provide a natural evolution in responding to the strengths and limitations of their present efforts.

Why Place-Based Community Engagement?

Place-based community engagement offers a promising strategy to respond to the changing context of higher education in order to more fully maximize university and community resources for deep and lasting social change. A place-based community engagement framework builds upon the evolution of community engagement in higher education by providing campuses and communities with many significant mutual benefits.

Centralized Strategy

Utilizing a place-based community engagement framework presents universities and their community partners with a centralized strategy to pursue long-term change on campus and in the community. In developing community engagement strategies, most universities and community organizations face significant challenges in deciding with whom to partner and why. Frequently this leads universities and community organizations to say yes to too many opportunities, significantly limiting their ability to pursue long-term impact. Focusing on an established geographic area can make it much easier to decide where to deploy university and community resources and which partnerships to prioritize. By narrowing their focus, universities and community partners may increase their ability to form strong and sustainable partnerships that are of greater value to all stakeholders.

Enhanced Visibility

Place-based community engagement can provide universities with a central coherent narrative for communicating their commitment to engaging in the wider community. Having one major community engagement story to tell, instead of dozens of disparate smaller vignettes, may enable campuses to attain much greater external visibility among alumni, community organizations, and elected officials. Community organizations that are partnering with universities engaged in place-based efforts can also increase their visibility, as they can collaborate with their university partner on messaging, communication strategy, and storytelling.

Potential for More Funding

In a time of scarce resources, universities that utilize a place-based community engagement approach can increase their likelihood of attracting additional financial support from foundations, corporations, individuals, and public partners. As noted earlier in this chapter, the current predominant university community engagement model tends to focus much more on the learning experiences of college students rather than on community impact. Since many funders want to maximize their impact, they may find this approach less appealing. Placing more of an equal emphasis on the campus and the community may expand the potential to attain additional financial support.

Many funders, especially more established regional and national funding institutions, seek big ideas that can demonstrate measurable results. Place-based community engagement can offer a chance for funders to invest in significant long-term efforts that focus equally on campus and community impact. For community organizations, this may lead funders to make larger and more sustainable direct investments in their programs. For universities, funders may provide support for the university to play a role of convener, as funders place value in efforts to orchestrate the work of multiple organizations. Finally, the long-term and bold vision presented by place-based community engagement initiatives can entice funders to make more sizable investments in the collaborative of university and community partners.

Expanded Community Partnerships

The long-term focused nature of place-based community engagement presents a chance for campus and community leaders to deepen and enhance partnerships. Knowing that the university has made a long-term commitment to support their mission and build their organizational capacity, community partners may be more likely to commit staff and other resources to develop relationships with university faculty and staff. As relationships between campus and community leaders strengthen, the depth and sophistication of shared projects can grow, blurring the lines among organizational mission, systems, and structures to attain stronger results.

Support for Admissions and Enrollment Management

Place-based community engagement can be a competitive enrollment advantage. Through their place-based community engagement initiatives, universities can, in partnership with donors, develop scholarship opportunities to attract students from the initiative's geographic area to attend the institution. In addition, by messaging their expansive commitment to community engagement, universities can attract prospective students who seek learning environments where they can enhance their skills and abilities to lead and work for positive social change. In some cases, prospective students who reside locally (including students who reside within the boundaries of a place-based initiative) may also be attracted to the university due to their positive experience with the university as K–12 students and/or desire to serve their own community as college students.

Stronger University Learning Environments

A significant challenge of many campus community engagement efforts is the sporadic nature of engaging college students. Connecting community engagement to courses has great benefit but often, after the end of the academic term, student involvement at community sites can wane. Place-based community engagement can increase the likelihood of students making a multiterm commitment to serve and learn in one geographic area. Courses, volunteer opportunities, community service work-study offerings, and other approaches to community engagement can be threaded together to offer students an opportunity to experience a sense of place over a long period of time. This increased duration and intensity of student engagement can significantly enhance student learning experiences (Eyler & Giles, 1999).

In addition to supporting student-driven engagement, the geographic focus of a place-based strategy may offer university faculty an opportunity to focus their community-engaged research and teaching, especially with incentivized opportunities. By focusing on one place, faculty can better understand the history and current context of the neighborhood(s) and cultivate stronger long-term community partnerships. With more knowledge and more robust partnerships, faculty can provide richer community-oriented learning experiences for their students. The increased awareness of context, history, and partnerships can also augment faculty research opportunities.

Cultivating a Sense of Place

One dominant feature of most colleges and universities is that they are rooted in a geographic place. Frequently, institutions have existed in the same location for decades and even centuries. Although they may create additional branches or international campuses, rarely do institutions of higher education physically move locations. Many institutions, by intention or by happenstance, have literally or metaphorically walled themselves off from their wider communities. Sadly, this has often led to contentious relationships with local communities as well as contributed to real and perceived actions by the university that are harmful to the wider community. Place-based community engagement invites the institution of higher education to more deeply connect to its sense of place. By positively embracing their geographic location, universities and colleges can strengthen their role as a positive force within their wider community context.

Opportunity to More Fully Pursue Racial Equity

The persistence of racism within our universities and in our communities challenges institutions of higher education to think critically and act thoughtfully in pursuit of a vision of racial equity. Many contemporary approaches to community engagement in higher education employ a transactional model of campus and community partnerships that limits the potential for transformation (Stoecker, 2016). Although they offer glimpses of a more just world, these short-term and often superficial campus and community connections do little to address systemic societal issues. This is particularly true in considering how community engagement in higher education, in particular on predominantly White campuses, can more fully contest racism.

In focusing on long-term partnerships within a specific geographic area, universities pursuing place-based engagement have an opportunity to more fully understand the history of race and racism in their communities. Enduring consistent relationships between campus and community leaders can invite opportunities to more fully unpack issues of power and privilege related to social issues such as racism and systemic social inequalities. Moreover, the quick feedback loops inherent in the intensive place-based approach may allow leaders to swiftly address issues in real time, specifically issues arising from unexplored assumptions and biases of race and racism.

Long-Term Significant Transformation

Frequently, university-community partnerships focus on highly visible events and one-time projects, such as a service day, that offer the university a way of celebrating its commitment to connecting with its wider community. Although these opportunities can build a sense of community, their short duration and low time commitment can limit their long-term impact on the campus and the community. Place-based community engagement invites university and community leaders to pursue a longer-term vision of transformation.

Institutional and community change is a long and often nonlinear process. By intensely focusing campus and community partnerships within one geographic area, campus and community institutions and organizations can establish longer-term shared visions, test different approaches, and make necessary adjustments. These processes are likely to increase trust among all stakeholders. Increased trust and long-term commitment can also enable partners to stay connected and engaged as they move through the pitfalls and challenges that naturally arise within any social change effort.

Differentiating Place-Based Community Engagement From Other Strategies

Many institutions of higher education are committed to community engagement through a variety of distinct strategies. As noted earlier, hundreds of universities and colleges continue to utilize service-learning as a pedagogical and engagement strategy with strong support from centralized campus offices and organizations like Campus Compact. Other institutions have become actively involved in the burgeoning anchor institution movement, embracing their sense of place to contribute economically and in other ways to their surrounding communities. Place-based community engagement is complementary to but different from these other major engagement strategies.

Place-Based Community Engagement Differs From Service-Learning Pedagogy

Place-based community engagement frequently draws upon the process and practice of service-learning. Yet it is not the same as traditional service-learning approaches. Place-based community engagement offers a more expansive and unified platform for campus-wide engagement.

For example, in a traditional service-learning context an individual faculty member may work with community partners to integrate a service opportunity within his or her course to enhance the course content. With place-based community engagement, this individual will be one of many faculty members (and campus stakeholders) who engage with a coalition of community partners in a particular geographic area to advance student learning and community impact. In other words, the faculty member is working within a larger web of the campus community with a network of local partners to pursue mutual benefit. In short, place-based community engagement moves service-learning from isolated individual actions to an institution-wide strategy embracing long-term reciprocal community partnerships.

Place-Based Community Engagement Differs From Anchor Institutions

Recent years have seen a surge of interest in the university as an anchor institution. *Anchor institutions* are defined as organizations that, once established in a location, are not likely to leave (Dubb, McKinley, & Howard, 2013). The anchor institution movement focuses on harnessing the economic power of large place-bound nonprofit institutions, particularly universities and hospitals, to support local economies through local employment, community-based investment, and locally sourced procurement strategies (Dubb et al., 2013).

Place-based and anchor institution strategies overlap in how they can expand the community-facing roles of the university to include convening community and campus organizations, advocating for community issues, and on occasion even funding community needs. In some cases, institutions pursuing a place-based community engagement strategy may also see themselves as anchor institutions, but the two are not the exact same thing.

An anchor institution strategy often significantly highlights the university's economic development portfolio, which receives less emphasis in most place-based approaches. In addition, place-based engagement usually focuses on a smaller geographic area than an anchor institution approach. Finally, anchor institution strategies often originate from the university's central administration, quite frequently the finance and business offices. Place-based engagement draws leadership from both high-level university administrators and also grassroots community and campus members.

Place-Based Community Engagement: What Does It Look Like in Practice?

As we have explored in this chapter, place-based community engagement provides universities with a strategy to respond to the changing context of higher education and the evolving field of community engagement. If pursued thoughtfully, place-based community engagement can provide universities and their communities with many significant additional benefits. Yet what exactly does place-based community engagement look like in practice? How is *place-based engagement* defined? And what are the considerations for creating and pursuing an initiative? In chapter 2 we examine these questions by exploring place-based community engagement in practice.

2

PLACE-BASED COMMUNITY ENGAGEMENT IN PRACTICE

O ver the past two decades, community engagement that focuses on a specific geographic area has gained prominence in a number of contexts throughout the United States. In the early 2000s the Harlem Children's Zone led by Geoffrey Canada gained widespread notoriety. Canada's concept was both simple and remarkably complex. Focus programs and support structures intensely on a specific geographic area and do everything possible to enable children and youth to succeed. Initially, the Harlem Children's Zone focused on just a few blocks of Harlem; then it expanded to several dozen and today it encompasses almost 100 blocks and supports over 10,000 children (Harlem Children's Zone, n.d.).

At the same time as the Harlem Children's Zone rose to prominence, major philanthropies like the Skillman Foundation, C.F. Foundation, and the MacArthur Foundation also invested significant financial resources in intensive neighborhood-based initiatives (Burns & Brown, 2012). In 2000 the Annie E. Casey Foundation launched its Making Connections initiative that invested in 22 communities throughout the country to support neighborhood-based change efforts utilizing interconnected strategies of education, health, housing, and economic opportunity (Feister, 2011).

Noting the success of the Harlem Children's Zone and the examples of major foundations, the Obama administration utilized federal funding to incentivize communities throughout the country to draw upon lessons learned from Harlem and other communities to pursue positive change for thousands of children and families. Through the Department of Education's Promise Neighborhood Initiative and the Department of Housing and Urban Development's Choice Neighborhood Initiative dozens of communities received millions of dollars. The multiyear funding helped create comprehensive initiatives that linked education, housing, health, and economic opportunity to build the capacity of some of our nation's most marginalized neighborhoods.

The national evolution of the place-based approach has led a growing number of higher education institutions to adopt the concept in their local communities. This chapter focuses on place-based community engagement in practice, particularly in the context of higher education. First, we provide a few examples of universities that are engaged in place-based work in various locations in the United States and Canada. We subsequently define *place-based community engagement* and then provide a three-phase framework for place-based community engagement in practice.

Universities and Place-Based Initiatives

With the high visibility of national place-based efforts such as the Harlem Children's Zone, in recent years dozens of universities and colleges across the United States and Canada have begun to utilize a place-based approach to drive their community engagement efforts. The look and feel of each institution's approach can vary significantly depending on its institutional and community context. Geography, institutional type, motivations, and economic factors significantly influence how various institutions approach place-based engagement.

For example, many urban universities are pursuing place-based engagement to connect with their neighborhoods and communities, as in the following:

- Fairfield University is embarking on a place-based initiative focusing on educational initiatives at a local K–8 school in Bridgeport, Connecticut. The partnership has grown from its initial focus on tutoring to a more holistic partnership including counseling, school psychology, and educational technology (Seattle University Place-Based Institute, 2016).
- Loyola University Chicago has recently launched a place-based initiative in the communities adjacent to its campus in Chicago, Illinois. The enhanced partnerships are mobilizing faculty, staff, and students to focus on issues of health and education within neighborhood schools of Rogers Park, Edgewater, and Uptown (Seattle University Place-Based Institute, 2016).
- Santa Clara University has a Thriving Neighbors Initiative that focuses engaged scholarship and teaching initiatives on five neighborhoods encompassing the Greater Washington community in San Jose, California. The initiative connects faculty, staff, and students with local residents, organizations, businesses, and community leaders

in areas of health, education, and entrepreneurship (Santa Clara University Ignatian Center for Jesuit Education, n.d.).

- The University of Pittsburgh recently announced a strategy of developing new Centers for Urban Engagement in partnership with local neighborhood leaders and organizations near its campus in Pittsburgh, Pennsylvania (University of Pittsburgh, 2016). Each center will have a neighborhood ambassador to facilitate deeper connections between the campus and community.

Institutions in smaller cities as well as suburban and rural areas are also pursuing place-based strategies, as in the following examples:

- The University of New Brunswick Saint John in Canada is implementing the Promise Partnership that mobilizes university students to serve as tutors and mentors in several K–12 schools in the small city of Saint John (population 67,675). Since 2010, the partnership has utilized comprehensive evaluation metrics to measure impact and drive program modifications (University of New Brunswick, n.d.).
- Pacific Lutheran University located in Parkland, Washington, an unincorporated area outside of Tacoma, has launched the Parkland Education Initiative "to connect local K–8 youth with college students through meaningful relationships and learning" (Pacific Lutheran University, n.d.). Pacific Lutheran students serve as mentors and tutors at four nearby elementary schools and one neighborhood middle school.
- Berea College is pursuing an expansive county-wide place-based effort called Berea College Partners for Education. With funding from a federal Promise Neighborhood grant, this effort focuses on education and support services for over 10,000 students living in 386 square miles of rural Knox County, Kentucky (Broader, Bolder Approach to Education, n.d.).

A wide variety of influences lead universities and colleges to pursue place-based community engagement. Sometimes significant external factors are the drivers, as seen in the following examples:

- Grand Canyon University is pursuing a goal of neighborhood revitalization. Grand Canyon University's United by Purpose project is centered on the transformation of a neighborhood adjacent to its campus in West Phoenix, Arizona. The project focuses on education, crime prevention, job development, and residential property renewal.

United by Purpose includes an innovative "Learning Lounge" where local high school students receive academic support on the GCU campus (United by Purpose, n.d.).

- The University of San Francisco is striving to mitigate the displacement of communities of color in San Francisco, California. The university launched Engage San Francisco to support residents of San Francisco's Western Addition who are being negatively impacted by the crisis of affordability and the ensuing outmigration from the city. Housed in the Leo T. McCarthy Center for Public Service and Common Good, Engage San Francisco mobilizes academic departments and students to promote community-identified outcomes in areas of affordable housing, health, education, and employment (University of San Francisco, n.d.).

And at other times, internal university and college factors provide the spark:

- Whitworth University has focused its community engagement efforts on the West Central neighborhood of Spokane, Washington, located about seven miles from campus. Grounded in its religious identity, Whitworth has drawn upon the vision of Christian Community Development to partner with neighborhood organizations and residents through service-learning; university research; and, more recently, capital resources and procurement efforts (Seattle University Place-Based Institute, 2016). The university's Dornsife Center provides a centralized hub for coordination of campus and community partnerships.
- Regis University has launched Cultivate Health to connect its health-related academic programs to surrounding neighborhoods in Denver, Colorado. Cultivate Health is a campus-community partnership connecting Regis with neighborhood residents and nonprofit partners to "promote health in the environments in which we live, work and learn" (Seattle University Place-Based Institute, 2016). Supported by a major grant from the Colorado Health Foundation, the project focuses on supporting the health and wellness of over 14,000 residents living in neighborhoods adjacent to the campus through programs and system innovations addressing a variety of health issues.

With such a wide variance in geographic context, motivating factors, and countless other influencers, there is not one universal model of a university place-based community engagement strategy. This invites almost any type of institution to explore a place-based approach and adapt it to its specific campus and community context. This also suggests that institutions should conduct a thoughtful analysis of their specific circumstances in order to craft a vision and plan that will lead to success.

Defining *Place-Based Community Engagement*

The absence of a set prototype for a place-based community engagement initiative does not mean that these initiatives operate without definition. Most place-based community engagement initiatives draw upon a few specific guidelines and tenets.

We define *place-based community engagement* in higher education as a long-term university-wide commitment to partner with local residents, organizations, and other leaders to focus equally on campus and community impact within a clearly defined geographic area (see Table 2.1). Within this definition we highlight several key principles.

A Geographic Focus

Place-based community engagement focuses intensively on a clear and definable geographic area. This enables the university to more intentionally concentrate its partnerships on specific communities and neighborhood residents, organizations, and businesses. The focus on one "place" also invites the campus and community to utilize demographic data, historical material, and other information about the geographic area to inform their strategy and analysis. Finally, the geographic focus enables the university and community partners to clearly say "yes" to partnerships linked to the area of focus and "no" to opportunities that don't fit the geographic approach.

Many universities that are utilizing a place-based community engagement approach focus on neighborhoods and communities adjacent to or near their campus. This strategy offers a natural invitation for universities and their partners to explore what it means to be a "neighbor." In addition, it can narrow the gap between the "campus" and the "community" and even begin to blur the lines, creating a sense of the campus and community as one. Focusing on communities adjacent to campus also assists with logistical issues such as minimizing the transportation challenges of linking the campus and community.

Equal Emphasis on Campus and Community Impact

As described in chapter 1, faculty members' use of service-learning as a pedagogical strategy is increasing on many campuses, and many colleges and

TABLE 2.1

Place-Based Community Engagement

Definition	Key Concepts	Phases		
		Phase 1: Exploration	**Phase 2: Development**	**Phase 3: Sustaining**
A long-term university-wide commitment to partner with local residents, organizations, and other leaders to focus equally on campus and community impact within a clearly defined geographic area	1. A geographic focus 2. Equal emphasis on campus *and* community impact 3. Long-term vision and commitment 4. University-wide engagement that animates the mission and develops the institution 5. Drawing upon the concept of collective impact	• Catalyst • Leadership • Engaging campus and community • Geographic considerations: Identifying and exploring place • Organizational structures and systems: Key questions	• Programs and partnerships: Experimentation • Resources and funding: Increasing capacity • Organizational structures and personnel: Building infrastructure	• Geographic considerations: Responding to neighborhood change • Programs and partnerships: Moving toward sustainability • Resources and funding: Maturation of sources and greater stability of funding • Organizational structures and personnel: Succession and change management

universities continue to invest in expanding staffing and support for multiple forms of community engagement.

Although there are many examples of individual faculty and student-driven projects that focus significantly on community impact, most university-wide community engagement strategies place much greater emphasis on campus impact over community impact. As institutions whose primary focus is on university student learning, this emphasis on the campus is natural but also inhibits the opportunity for truly transformational partnerships.

Place-based community engagement invites universities to put an equal emphasis on campus *and* community impact. This balanced emphasis substantially increases the ability for the campus and community to collectively attain measurable and lasting results, both within the wider community and within the university. Equally emphasizing campus and community impact changes the traditional paradigm of campus-community partnerships, opening up many new possibilities for all stakeholders to explore.

Long-Term Vision and Commitment

Place-based community engagement efforts present a long-term vision and sustained commitment to partnership. Successful place-based approaches engage the campus and community in shared visioning exercises and lead to commitments that have no end date. This sense of permanency enables all campus and community stakeholders to change and adapt to new opportunities and emerging challenges, knowing that a steadfast pursuit of shared goals will remain.

University-Wide Engagement That Animates the Mission and Develops the Institution

Place-based community engagement efforts invite university-wide involvement and clearly focus on furthering the institution's purpose or mission. This includes institution-building efforts, especially for public institutions whose mission is to serve the residents of their states. This top-down and bottom-up approach can catalyze involvement among university students, faculty, staff, alumni, trustees, and senior administrators. Place-based efforts that only focus on one aspect of university engagement, such as individual faculty use of service-learning, can have success, but the most expansive change occurs when multiple parts of the university are collectively contributing to the place-based partnerships. This process can help an institution break down silos and avoid duplicative efforts. In addition, this multipronged approach to engagement increases the likelihood for sustainability as it invites various campus units to engage and be transformed through their involvement.

Drawing Upon the Concept of Collective Impact

Because of the multiple variables and many partners involved in place-based partnerships, the concept and practice of collective impact lend themselves well to place-based community engagement. Kania and Kramer (2011) define *collective impact* as "the commitment of a group of actors from different sectors to a common agenda for solving a specific social problem, using a structured form of collaboration" (p. 36). Conceptualized and popularized by the *Stanford Social Innovation Review,* collective impact involves five key elements: (a) a common goal, (b) shared measurement and use of impact data, (c) mutually reinforcing activities, (d) continuous communication, and (e) a strong backbone infrastructure (Kania & Kramer, 2011).

The process of collective impact can unite multiple campus and community offices, organizations, and stakeholders to pursue a common goal. Although getting multiple partners to work together is messy and sometimes cumbersome, the framework of collective impact presents universities and community partners pursuing place-based partnerships with an organizing strategy and process to guide their planning, implementation, and evaluation efforts. In addition, in many cases the university can serve as a natural "backbone" organization and attract external funding to support this important role.

Moving From Theory to Practice: Three Phases of Place-Based Community Engagement

Implementing a place-based community engagement initiative on a university campus takes time and careful planning. The complexity of a university campus and the diffused nature of decision-making call for the involvement of many stakeholders and the inclusion of leadership at all levels of the university. This need for an intentional and thoughtful process also extends into the community with attentiveness to specific community dynamics and a significant emphasis on listening overtaking immediate action. In addition, each institution's and community's unique cultural, historical, community, and organizational context also shapes an initiative.

Through our multiple case study approach, we identified three distinct phases of place-based community engagement: (a) exploration, (b) development, and (c) sustaining.

Phase One: Exploration

Frequently, campuses begin to consider a place-based community engagement initiative because of a catalyzing event or issue. A catalyst, such as a change in presidential leadership or interest of a major donor, can arise from within the university. Conversely, external university factors such as safety issues, a funding opportunity, changing economic forces, or shifting community demographics may provide a catalyst. This phase involves many stakeholders, especially senior university leadership, current and potential campus and community partners, and existing community engagement offices and staff. The exploration phase may be brief or quite long—this often depends on whether the university president offers a directive, which leads to a short exploration period, or whether the initiative is driven by a bottom-up organizational strategy, which typically has a longer process.

The central considerations of the exploration phase are whether the institution should take on a university-wide community engagement initiative and, if so, what shape and form it should take. The pivotal point that marks the end of this phase is a decision whether or not to proceed with a university-wide community engagement initiative. Our study identified several key areas that are pertinent to the exploration phase, including leadership, engaging campus and community, geographic considerations, and organizational structures and systems.

Leadership

During the exploration phase, senior university leadership such as the president, provost, and director of a community engagement office are typically the key decision makers. These individuals often lead the effort to get buy-in and support from trustees, deans, donors, faculty, staff, and students. For some institutions, a president may utilize community engagement as a key platform for guiding the university. Yet senior leadership is not always paramount. Some institutions may have more of a grassroots exploratory approach in which faculty, staff, and students grow an idea and take it to senior university leadership. During the exploration phase a representative body of the university will likely begin to engage with campus and community stakeholders in envisioning the size and scope of the initiative.

Engaging Campus and Community

A community engagement initiative requires consistent and deep participation from the university and its wider communities. During the exploration phase, engagement with key campus stakeholders is paramount. For campuses with cultures and traditions of more formal university-wide processes, an official group may convene and develop a plan for engagement. For institutions with less formalized processes and cultures, the exploration phase looks and feels more organic, with less prescribed discussion arising among groups on and off campus.

Regardless of an institution's penchant for formality, the exploration phase involves better understanding the partnerships and campus-community connections that already exist in order to see a fuller picture of what may be possible. During this period, university representatives frequently engage with the greater community, developing deeper understandings of community perspectives and existing partnerships. Some institutions may also reach out to organizations and institutions that they have yet to partner with to understand opportunities for possible new collaborations. The back-and-forth discussions between campus and community are often guided by questions such as what more could be possible and what it would take to have greater shared impact.

Geographic Considerations: Identifying and Exploring Place
The exploration phase includes an analysis and identification of the geographic focus of the initiative. For some institutions, this focus may stem from existing community partnerships or collaboratives. For others, it may be based on an attendance zone of a public school or a school feeder pattern (e.g., elementary school, middle school, and high school). The proximity to campus is frequently a key consideration in solidifying the geographic emphasis for an initiative.

Most universities exploring a place-based initiative are motivated to positively impact economic or social community needs, such as economic inequality, lack of job opportunities, or underresourced and underperforming schools. Given the history of racial segregation and racism in the United States and the inherent connection to economic and educational inequality, many universities end up pursuing place-based initiatives with communities that are racially different from the predominant populations of their institutions. For example, although all five of the universities profiled in this book are racially diverse (some more than others), they are all historically White campuses with a predominantly White student population. The issues of power and privilege that arise from this racial dynamic are important considerations to examine during the exploratory phase.

Organizational Structures and Systems: Key Questions
During the exploration phase it is important to examine existing university structures, staffing, and resources in order to position the place-based initiative for long-term success. There are several important structural, personnel, and financial questions to investigate, including the following:

- Who will be responsible for the initiative and where might it be housed (academic affairs, student affairs, or community relations)?

- What does the leadership structure look like? Does an existing campus leader take on this role? Is someone new hired?
- Is there an opportunity to combine several existing offices/departments to maximize university-wide engagement?
- What are the funding resources to draw upon in order to launch and implement the initiative? Are any individuals or foundations in a position to provide immediate support?

For community engagement offices, this is often a time for evaluating the opportunities and limitations of the current organizational configuration. Questions that often emerge include the following:

- What is the capacity of the current organizational structure and staff to pursue a place-based initiative?
- Where is there potential for growth among individuals or in the organization?
- How does the office continue with existing partnerships while expanding and deepening its commitment to partnerships related to the place-based initiative?
- Where might the office scale back partnerships or reexamine partnerships that are not currently working well?

Some campuses may also examine their own physical space and proximity to the community and consider questions such as the following:

- Is there enough space to accommodate staffing growth/new demands for office and meeting space?
- Where are the campus leaders of the initiative housed in proximity to the community?
- How accessible is the space to the community?

Phase Two: Development

Once there is a commitment to start an initiative, the development phase begins. This phase involves significant experimentation with opportunities to quickly pursue new ideas, projects, and partnerships. During this phase, change and transition become normative as new partnerships and programs begin and existing partnerships and programs start to rapidly innovate. For staff working on the initiative, this is a time of excitement, change, and also immense transition. Some staff may shift and change roles whereas others may decide to leave their positions to pursue other options.

The development phase usually involves the tracking and reporting of initial measurable results which serve as indicators of success and change. A pivotal point that marks the end of this phase is when general awareness of the initiative saturates the university and wider community. Key areas of the development phase include programs and partnerships, organizational structures and personnel, and resources and funding.

Programs and Partnerships: Experimentation

For campus-community partnerships and programs this is the exciting period of experimentation. The exploration phase brings new collaborations and new partnerships and sometimes rapid growth. In order to deepen partnerships and strengthen trust, initiative leaders must be carefully attentive to campus and community issues that may quickly arise.

Often the enthusiasm and excitement of this period leads to a greater focus on quantity rather than quality of programs. Within the university, new financial incentives such as fellowships or grants are frequently presented to faculty and staff in order to deepen involvement in the initiative. Some of these incentives may focus on building new partnerships and/or better aligning existing partnerships with the university's new initiative. For the community, the exploration phase brings new opportunities to engage in planning and visioning conversations in order to deepen and expand partnerships to address community needs. For initiatives working with schools, this is often a time of rapid program and partnership development with elementary schools.

Data-informed decision-making is central to the development phase, as campus and community partners review current practices and decide what to build upon and what to close out. In certain instances, the university may pivot away from some of its existing community partnerships that do not align with its place-based approach. Careful diplomacy and forethought is essential in navigating these shifts in focus.

Organizational Structures and Personnel: Building Infrastructure

Along with the rapid development of partnerships and programs, the development phase brings significant movement in aligning organizational structures and staffing to maximize the success of the initiative. Staffing structures may shift with the addition of senior-level leadership or the elevation of current staff in order to better facilitate the initiative. Often, increasing visibility and job responsibilities lead directors of community engagement offices to become executive directors, a title that better reflects the community-facing nature of these positions and that may be better understood by external partners.

Program-oriented community engagement staff may also experience shifts in their job descriptions with new titles and changing roles. For nimble staff members, whose talents and interests align with these shifts, the change can be exciting and welcomed. One of the challenges of the development phase is that the rapid pace of change and lack of total role clarity can challenge staff who may not have the acumen or passion for the needs of the new organizational landscape. Some staff members, either by choice or because of changing organizational needs, may decide not to stay in their roles.

Consistent with the increased focus on community, some campuses may decide to change the names of their community engagement offices to better reflect the shift in their mission and focus. In addition, some campuses may also opt to change the physical locations of their community engagement office(s), possibly moving to parts of campus that make it easier to connect and partner with the community.

Resources and Funding: Increasing Capacity

Given the rapid growth in programs, partnerships, and organizational structures, the need for additional funding becomes increasingly important during the development phase. In many cases, community engagement and fund development staff step up efforts to pursue grant opportunities. In addition to pursuing external funding, university leaders often allocate new or redistribute existing university resources to support the new place-based effort. Often the university will allocate a development officer or grant-writer to identify and cultivate existing or prospective funders who may be interested in the place-based approach.

Phase Three: Sustaining

After the experimental and somewhat chaotic period of the development phase, the sustaining phase brings a more measured pace of change and a more focused and confident growth of the initiative. During this phase moving partnerships and programs toward financial and organizational sustainability becomes a central priority. In addition, success in acquiring funding can lead to more confidence in a long-term business and program model. Programmatically, emerging community issues may shift the geographic focus of the place-based initiative or call for new ways of connecting the university to the community. Organizationally, structural and staffing systems have likely become more stable, and it becomes easier to plan for succession and staffing transitions should they arise.

In this phase, the following are several key indicators that the initiative is moving toward long-term sustainability:

- The university integrates the initiative into its strategic plan.
- Opportunities for faculty and students to engage in the initiative become more and more institutionalized within academic departments and other campus units.
- Funders begin to seek the university and its community partners out because of the strong track record of innovation, collective impact, and measurable success.
- The university funds scholarships for students from the initiative's geographic area to attend the university.
- A pattern of "homegrown leadership" arises whereby individuals from the neighborhood graduate from the university and return to their community to take on leadership roles.

Geographic Considerations: Responding to Neighborhood Change
During the sustaining phase, the geographic focus of the place-based initiative remains a central tenet of the community engagement strategy, yet external forces may begin to impact the composition of the community. For example, changes in the neighborhood arising from development and/or redevelopment may impact where people are living and who is living in the neighborhood. Changes within the P–12 school system such as shifts in school boundaries, the opening and closing of schools, and shifts in school policy such as school start times may impact partnerships with campus programs and campus units.

Programs and Partnerships: Moving Toward Sustainability
Entering the sustainability phase frequently leads campus-community partnerships to a point of greater maturation and stability. In many cases the focus on the quantity of programs and partnerships begins to subside and quality becomes much more of a priority. For example, campuses in this phase often become more focused on the preparation of college students to engage more critically and effectively instead of simply getting lots of students out to serve in the neighborhood. In addition, once programs have operated for several years, data and evaluation results provide significant information to improve programs and, in some cases, lead to decisions to sunset activities. For initiatives that have a major focus on school partnerships and have a pipeline approach, this phase may mean expanding partnerships from elementary schools to middle and/or high schools. A central challenge for initiatives that have entered the sustainability phase is balancing the need for continuity of campus-community partnerships with the imperative of remaining relevant, responsive, and innovative.

Resources and Funding: Maturation of Sources and Greater Stability of Funding
Financially, the phase of sustainability can lead to greater stability and pre-
dictability for funding streams. As the initiative reports results and demonstrates success in mobilizing the campus and community, confidence in
seeking and securing funding typically grows, although the pressure to maintain and expand funding likely persists. In addition, funding partners who
have shown modest support during the initial phases may begin to make
larger and longer-term investments as they have more confidence in the long-
term trajectory of the initiative. Finally, within the university, some campus
partners (colleges, academic departments, other offices) may begin to make
financial and resource investments in specific aspects of the initiative.

Organizational Structures and Personnel: Succession and Change Management
As the initiative continues to develop, so does its organizational structure.
A slower pace of organizational growth may allow leaders of place-based
efforts to provide additional training and resources to new and existing staff
to manage the change process that has become the new normal. Often leaders will also develop a succession plan to address any anticipated and/or
unanticipated changes in staffing and leadership. As the larger and more
sophisticated organization begins to mature and stabilize, some staff may also
recognize, on their own or through discussions with their supervisors, that
their gifts and passions no longer fit the needs of the evolving organization,
leading them to decide to pursue other professional opportunities.

Place-Based Community Engagement in Practice: A Deeper Look

As this chapter illustrates, universities and colleges that pursue place-based
community engagement often draw upon a common set of principles and
frequently move naturally through three phases of organizational growth.
In the next chapter, we will share more about the methodology we used and
provide a profile of the five place-based community engagement initiatives
that we will draw upon during the remainder of the book.

METHODOLOGY AND
INSTITUTIONAL PROFILES

U niversities and colleges that have effectively launched and sustained place-based community engagement initiatives can provide many lessons for institutions wanting to explore the approach. In this chapter, we will present the methodology we used to examine these five institutions and their initiatives, including a detailed understanding of the data we collected, analyzed, and interpreted. After describing the methodology, we will introduce each of the five initiatives, providing institutional context, noting how each initiative began, and highlighting some key components of each initiative.

Methodology

To advance our understanding and practice of place-based community engagement, the following three questions guided the development of this book:

1. What is place-based community engagement?
2. How is it being used in higher education?
3. What are key lessons learned from this strategy that advance positive social change?

To explore these questions, we used a multiple case study approach (Baxter & Jack, 2008), also known as a collective case study approach (Stake, 1995). We thought this approach was most appropriate as it allowed us to conduct in-depth case analysis and cross-case analysis on place-based community engagement at various institutions of higher education. Our method for binding our case (Stake, 1995; Yin, 2003) was to focus on existing place-based initiatives that have achieved a point of maturation (e.g., initiatives that have moved through a start-up period and attained some form of stability). We are assuming that although place-based community engagement initiatives at various institutions may have some similarities, there may be distinct cross-case differences due to multiple contextual factors such as the organizational culture and environment of the university, the type and scope of campus-community partnerships, and the geographic location of the university and its partner neighborhood.

Site Selection

In determining which sites to include in our case studies we examined the existing literature on university-community engagement strategies and focused on those that were geographically based in nature (Koth, 2013). In addition, we drew upon a series of 2-day institutes which had engaged over 20 institutions that were pursuing or considering a place-based community engagement strategy. We also consulted with colleagues in philanthropy, government, and public policy to identify additional campuses engaged in place-based efforts. In total, these various approaches identified 35 institutions.

After identifying an initial set of institutions, we narrowed the list of prospective case studies to 20 institutions which had reached a level of success and maturation in their place-based approach. We chose these more seasoned initiatives to allow us to showcase and describe the various phases of place-based community engagement that an institution typically goes through. In order to expand the number and examples of place-based engagement within the literature, we also decided not to include institutions that other publications had already showcased (e.g., Hodges & Dubb, 2012).

In making final decisions about which institutions to include we chose to emphasize institutions of various types. This included public and private institutions, institutions of variable sizes, and institutions from different Carnegie Classifications. We also chose institutions that would exemplify different approaches to place-based community engagement and institutions that pursued distinctive ways to fund their initiatives. The five institutions we chose were Drexel University, Loyola University Maryland, San Diego State University, Seattle University, and the University of San Diego.

Data Collection and Analysis

We engaged in a systematic process to gather information and data to conduct robust analysis to highlight promising practices and lessons learned from institutions engaged in place-based community engagement. We utilized two forms of data collection: document acquisition and in-depth analysis both prior to and subsequent to site visits. Upon completion of our site visits, we performed in-depth analysis of our meetings, conversations, and site notes.

Document Acquisition and Analysis

Document acquisition and analysis were important first steps in our research (Creswell, 2013). We completed a thorough review and document analysis of each initiative's public materials via their websites. In addition, we examined each institution's strategic plans and reviewed internal reports or other public documents that participants shared with us. For example, we reviewed an inaugural speech, several executive reports, and several grant proposals. Of the five institutions that we profiled, all but one campus (San Diego State University) received Presidential Honor Roll recognition. We reviewed the Honor Roll applications, which provided detailed information on outcomes and impact of service and service-learning efforts as well as other forms of community engagement.

Site Visits

We conducted intensive site visits at each of the five institutions profiled in this book. Prior to each visit we conducted a phone meeting with the lead from each institution. In this previsit conversation, we discussed the initiative to ensure that it fit our definition of *place-based community engagement.* We then discussed the possibility of visiting and our desire to meet with stakeholders from the university, community, and K–12 schools (if applicable). We also sent our main contact a copy of the questions we would seek to answer during our visit. Finally, we asked for any materials the institution thought would be beneficial to review before our visit.

During our site visits we met with a variety of stakeholders to gain a deeper perspective on each initiative. In small groups or one-on-one we met with university faculty, staff, and students; school counselors, principals, and teachers; community residents; funders; and a city councilperson. In total, we had conversations with approximately 190 stakeholders: 50 formal initiative staff members, 55 additional campus stakeholders, and 85 community members. For one site, San Diego State University, we interviewed the former president, who played an instrumental role in initiating their place-based initiative.

During the site visits, we took detailed notes and, in some instances (with permission), tape-recorded and transcribed our conversations. After each site visit, we completed a debriefing meeting to discuss our visits. We shared our notes with each other and had lengthy discussions on key lessons learned, tensions, and emergent practices (see Table 3.1). In this book, we cite institutional names and positions but leave out personal names,

TABLE 3.1
Site Visits

	Number of Initiative Staff Members	Number of On-Campus Members (faculty, staff, students)	Number of Community Members
Drexel University	5	15	25
Loyola University Maryland	14	5	11
San Diego State University	8	4	13
Seattle University	11	25	25
University of San Diego	12	6	11
Total	**50**	**55**	**85**

with the exception of university presidents (and presidents emeriti) and funders to highlight the positionality of the individuals while also providing some degree of confidentiality.

Data Analysis and Synthesis
In total, we completed four initial rounds of coding, followed by two rounds of thematic coding. We began an open coding process (Creswell, 2013) with our artifacts and notes. Thereafter, we conducted analysis drawing upon our framework of the three phases of an initiative (exploration, development, and sustaining). Within each phase, we conducted a round of pattern matching. Subsequently, we completed cross-case synthesis across institutions within each phase.

Last, we reviewed our data for two particular perspectives, assessment/outcomes and community partners. For the assessment/outcomes section we focused heavily on the initiatives' approaches to assessment and definitions of *success*. We also examined the community partner perspectives closely to gather viewpoints across sites that informed a collective set of lessons learned.

Trustworthiness

Trustworthiness is an important part of high-quality qualitative research (Creswell, 2013). We provided an opportunity for the stakeholders we met with to review our transcriptions (when applicable) and direct quotes. In addition, we completed peer debriefing to keep our biases as practitioners and faculty members in check.

Place-Based Engagement: Five Institutional Profiles

As described previously, for this project we reviewed and conducted cross-case analyses of five distinct universities that have successfully employed a place-based community engagement strategy. We chose these institutions to provide examples of place-based engagement in different institutional types, geographic locations, and community and campus contexts.

Drexel University

Founded in 1891 by philanthropist Anthony J. Drexel, Drexel University is a private research institution located in urban Philadelphia, Pennsylvania. Drexel's unique cooperative education program (known as Co-op) reflects its commitment to applied learning. As the university notes, "Through [the Co-op], students alternate periods of study with periods of full-time professional employment, providing unrivaled, valuable professional experience" (Drexel University, n.d.a). Drexel is also known as an early adopter of technology, as it was the first university that required students to have computers in 1983 and also has widely successful and long-running online degree programs. The university enrolls approximately 26,000 students in 13 colleges at the undergraduate and graduate levels.

Drexel has a long and expansive history of civic engagement that started with its cooperative education program. In 2003, the university created the Center for Civic Engagement, which provides students with opportunities to serve in local communities. In 2010, John Fry was appointed the president of Drexel. In his inaugural address, President Fry presented a vision for what would become Drexel's university-wide community engagement effort that today permeates all aspects of the university, including student service opportunities, faculty research, and economic development. To strategically engage in this work, in 2011, a vice provost for university and community partnerships was hired and serves as a member of the president's cabinet. In 2011, Drexel renamed the Center for Civic Engagement in honor of Philip B. Lindy, who provided a $15 million gift to advance the university's civic engagement efforts.

In 2012, the university created a strategic plan that centered community engagement as the vehicle to advance the university. Noted as an anchor institution strategy, Drexel's place-based initiative has six strategic goals: (a) improving safety and sustainability, (b) economic vitality, (c) health and wellness, (d) housing, (e) K–12 education, and (f) retail and arts (Drexel University Office of University and Community Partnerships, n.d.b). Drexel's place-based initiative is focused on two communities in the West

Philadelphia area: Mantua and Powelton Village. Mantua has a population of 12,956, a poverty rate of 43.2%, and an unemployment rate of 43.2% ("Crime in Philadelphia—Mantua," n.d.). Powelton Village, known for its Victorian homes, is located just northeast of the university (and just south of Mantua). Many Drexel, students live in Powelton Village, and the university owns properties in the area (see Figure 3.1).

At present, the Office of University and Community Partnerships oversees the four areas that advance Drexel's place-based initiative: Action for Early Learning (focuses on early childhood education efforts), Digital On-Ramps (workforce training efforts), the Dornsife Center (neighborhood hub for programming which serves as an extension center), and the Lindy Center for Civic Engagement (student service, service-learning, and community-based research opportunities). In addition to these areas of engagement, Drexel also offers a generous home purchasing program for employees of the university to obtain resources to buy homes in Mantua and Powelton Village.

In 2014, Drexel in conjunction with its community partners received a federal Promise Zone designation. In 2016, the federal government awarded Drexel, in partnership with the city of Philadelphia, the School District of Philadelphia, and several other organizations, a $30 million Promise Neighborhood grant. Through the grant, Drexel (which serves as the lead applicant) and the university's partners take a "cradle-to-career" approach to expand and strengthen early childhood education, family engagement, and teacher training.

Loyola University Maryland

Founded in 1852, Loyola University Maryland is a Jesuit Catholic university located in Baltimore, Maryland. Loyola Maryland's mission reflects its religious character and outlook:

> Loyola Maryland is committed to the educational and spiritual traditions of the Society of Jesus and to the ideals of liberal education and the development of the whole person. Accordingly, the University will inspire students to learn, lead, and serve in a diverse and changing world. (Loyola University Maryland, n.d.)

At present, Loyola Maryland has approximately 6,000 students enrolled in 35 undergraduate and 9 graduate programs. It has 4 different campuses: Evergreen campus (mainly undergraduates), Timonium and Columbia campuses (graduate students), and the Clinical Centers (focused on counseling, psychology, and health sciences) at the Belvedere Square and Columbia campuses. Father Brian Linnane has served as president since 2005.

Figure 3.1. Drexel place-based community engagement neighborhoods.

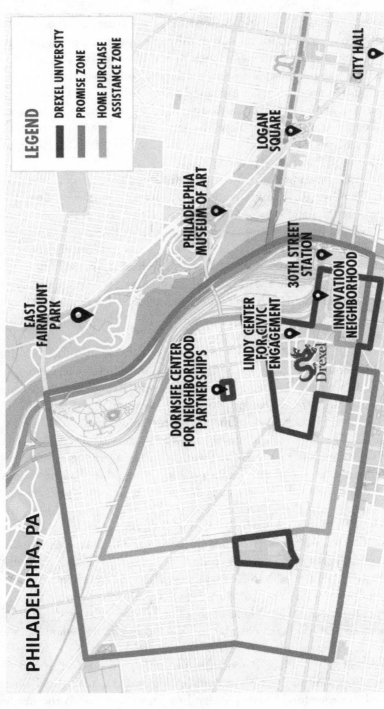

Note. Image courtesy of Drexel University. Used with permission.

In 2006, a few years into his tenure, President Linnane convened a task force consisting of stakeholders from all parts of the university to design and oversee the next steps for community engagement. The following year, the task force, co-led by the Government and Community Relations Office, worked with the American Friends Service Committee to develop Loyola is Listening, a survey tool to engage local residents living near the university's Evergreen Campus regarding area assets and opportunities for partnership with Loyola Maryland. At about the same time, community and campus members began developing a commercial plan for York Road, one of the neighborhood's primary thoroughfares.

Loyola Maryland's York Road Initiative was created as a result of this work. The York Road Initiative is a place-based community development strategy geographically focused in the York Road corridor communities of north Baltimore City adjacent to the university's Evergreen and Belvedere Square campuses (Figure 3.2). The initiative's mission is to collaborate with local residents as well as faith-based, civic, and business organizations to produce positive change in the York Road community (Seattle University Place-Based Institute, 2014). The initiative has four focus areas: (a) building civic capacity, (b) enhancing youth development, (c) strengthening the commercial corridor, and (d) food security.

Historically, York Road served as a main highway to connect Baltimore with Philadelphia. It has also served as a key boundary for residential segregation. As a recent *Baltimore Sun* article notes, "The division is clearest in northern Baltimore, where neighborhoods west of York Road—including Guilford and Homeland—are majority white and those east of the road—including Greater Govans and Northwood—are majority black" (Kim, 2015). In addition to the racial divide, there is a great economic divide; homes east of the road are significantly lower in value than homes on the west side of the road. Poverty rates are also significantly higher on the east side than the west (Yelp, 2015).

In 2010, Loyola Maryland hired a director to oversee the initiative. From 2010 to 2013, the York Road Initiative grew from an aspirational coalition of university partners to a community-based office with two full-time staff, two AmeriCorps VISTA members, and a cadre of student and resident volunteers. The York Road Initiative is reinforced through partnership support from Loyola Maryland's School of Education, the Sellinger School of Business and Management, the Clinical Centers at Belvedere Square, the Center for Community Service and Justice, and Loyola's Campus Ministry (Seattle University Place-Based Institute, 2014). In 2016, the staff of the Center for Community Service and Justice and the York Road Initiative merged in order for Loyola Maryland to better respond to the needs and assets of local community partners (Loyola Center for Community Service and Justice, n.d.).

The York Road Initiative has a variety of significant community partners. Strong City Baltimore, a major nonprofit in Baltimore, partners with Loyola Maryland to support Guilford Elementary/Middle School and Walter P. Carter Elementary School. The Govanstowne Business Association partners with Loyola Maryland to sponsor a farmers' market offering fresh produce to local residents. Through the York Corridor Collective, the university is partnering with elected officials and business leaders to form a new Business Improvement District. Finally, as a Jesuit Catholic institution, Loyola Maryland partners with several Catholic institutions, including the Baltimore Catholic Worker House and the St. Vincent De Paul Beans and Bread Center.

San Diego State University

Founded in 1897, San Diego State University is the oldest university in San Diego and 1 of 23 universities in the California State University system. San Diego State University currently has approximately 33,300 students in 190 different degree programs and is widely recognized as a leader in teacher preparation in the state of California. The university mission is "to provide research-oriented, high-quality education for undergraduate and graduate students and to contribute to the solution of problems through excellence and distinction in teaching, research, and service" (San Diego State University Office of the President, n.d.).

In 1996 Steven Weber became president of San Diego State University. During Weber's first year as president, Sol Price, founder of Price Club, the first membership-based warehouse store, approached him to be a higher education partner in addressing issues of crime and safety in City Heights, a neighborhood in central San Diego located about four miles southwest of the university (Price, 2012). From this initial meeting, San Diego State University, Price Philanthropies, the San Diego Unified School District, and numerous City Heights community organizations pursued multiple partnerships and projects in City Heights (see Figure 3.3). Sol Price through his philanthropic organization, Price Philanthropies, functioned as the primary funder and convener, and San Diego State University served as the primary higher education partner.

Compared to other universities that have pursued place-based community engagement, the San Diego State University initiative is unique in several ways. First, throughout the 20-year history of the initiative, the university has not served as the primary convener, as Price Philanthropies has fulfilled this role. In addition, during the initial years the president of the university, and

Figure 3.2. Loyola University Maryland: York Road initiative.

Loyola York Road Initiative Area

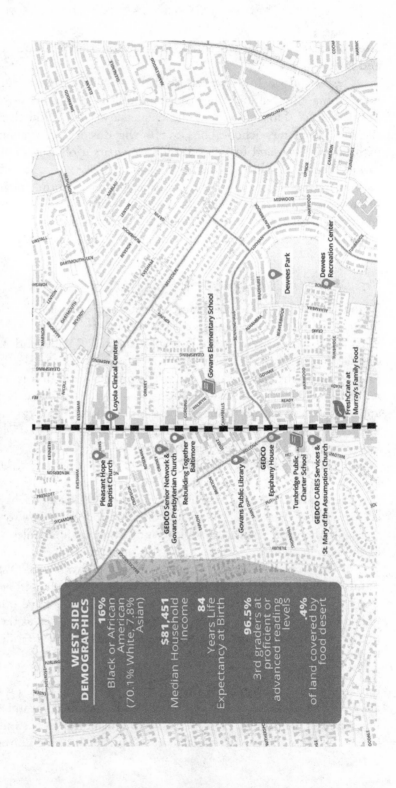

WEST SIDE
DEMOGRAPHICS

16%
Black or African
American
(70.1% White, 7.8%
Asian)

$81,451
Median Household
Income

84
Years Life
Expectancy at Birth

96.5%
3rd graders at
proficient or
advanced reading
levels

.4%
of land covered by
food desert

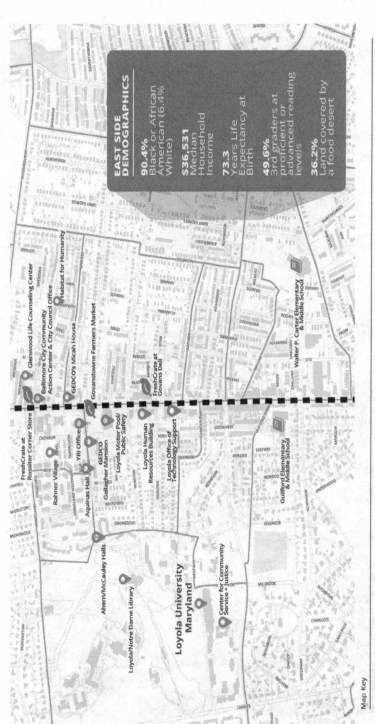

EAST SIDE DEMOGRAPHICS

90.4%
Black or African American (6.4% White)

$36,531
Median Household Income

73.3
Years Life Expectancy at Birth

49.6%
3rd graders at proficient or advanced reading levels

36.2%
Land covered by a food desert

N

Map Key

Loyola University Maryland Properties:
Center for Community Service and Justice
Loyola Office of Technology Support
Loyola Clinical Centers
Loyola Human Resources Building
Loyola Motor Pool / Public Safety
Loyola / Notre Dame Library
Loyola Office of Technology Support

Student Housing - Ahern / McCauley Halls
Student Housing - Aquinas Hall
Student Housing - Rahner Village
"YRI Office"- York Road Initiative, York Road Partnership & Strong City Baltimore Office

GEDCO: Govans Ecumenical Development Coorporation Properties

FreshCrate location
School
York Road
(~1.7 miles shown)

Source. Loyola University Maryland. Credit Julie Sayo. Used with permission.

Figure 3.3. San Diego State University place-based initiative, City Heights neighborhood.

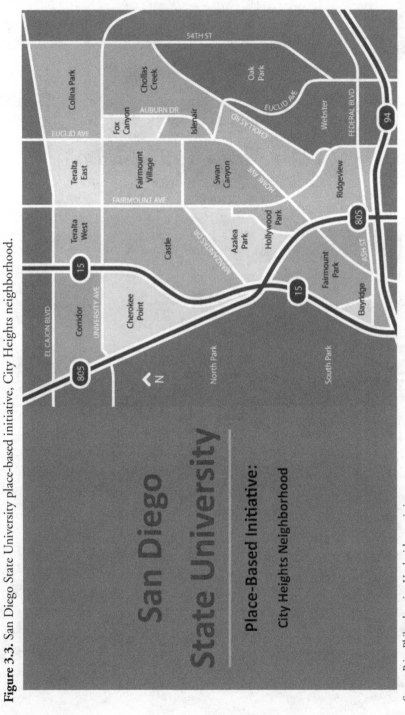

Source: Price Philanthropies. Used with permission.

not an existing office of community service/engagement, acted as the central university representative meeting with Sol Price and other San Diego leaders to develop the initiative. Once the work began, other university leaders guided the partnerships, including an associate provost for administration, the dean of the College of Education, and the director of the social work program.

Initially, the City Heights neighborhood developed as a typical suburban neighborhood for working and moderate-income families. After World War II and especially in the 1970s, City Heights became a neighborhood of immigrants and refugees (Price, 2012). In the 1990s, Mexican and Vietnamese immigrants comprised 2 of the largest populations in City Heights. Marcelli and Pastor (2015) note that from 2008 to 2012, 43% of the City Heights population lived in poverty (compared to San Diego County, which had a 23% poverty rate) and 73% of residents identified as Latino, Asian, or Black.

In the 1990s the City Heights neighborhood was cut in half with the building of a major new highway (Highway 15). At that time, a local newspaper labeled the neighborhood as the "crime capital of San Diego" (Burks, 2014). In addition, affordable and safe housing became a significant issue and neighborhood schools experienced declines in enrollment, with savvy parents sending their children to schools in other neighborhoods or districts. At this time, Sol Price convened many partners, including San Diego State University, to address resident and community needs (Martinez-Cosio & Bussell, 2013; Price, 2012).

With support from Price Philanthropies, San Diego State University's place-based community engagement efforts have concentrated primarily on educational partnerships with San Diego Unified School District schools in the City Heights neighborhood. The university has particularly focused on teacher training, educational interventions, and unique curricular opportunities that have involved P–12 teachers, City Heights children, and San Diego State University students. In addition, a unique scholarship program, the College Avenue Compact, provides college preparatory advising, parent education, and opportunities that, upon satisfying some basic requirements, provide City Heights students with guaranteed admission and a full academic scholarship to San Diego State University. Spanning almost two decades, San Diego State University's place-based work in City Heights represents the oldest place-based community engagement initiative profiled in this book.

Seattle University

Founded in 1891, Seattle University is a Jesuit Catholic university located on 50 acres in central Seattle. The university enrolls over 7,400 students in undergraduate and graduate programs within 9 distinct colleges and schools. Drawing upon its mission of "educating the whole person, to professional formation, and to empowering leaders for a just and humane world," Seattle University has a long history of service to society and advocating for social justice (Seattle University, n.d).

In 2004, the university created the Center for Community Engagement to centralize the coordination and strategic work of connecting the campus to the wider community through academic service-learning, volunteerism, community-based research, and other forms of community engagement. In 2007 a university trustee, Jim Sinegal, who had been impressed by the university's growing commitment to engaging its community, asked a simple question: "If Seattle University were to focus its community engagement efforts on a particular topic, neighborhood or issue, could it make more of a measurable impact on the community?" (J. Sinegal, personal communication, January 15, 2007).

Intrigued by the question and also moved by the university's recent hosting of a homeless encampment on campus, Seattle University president Stephen Sundborg asked a group of campus leaders to explore possible ideas and formulate a strategy. A university taskforce was created that engaged a variety of on- and off-campus stakeholders to develop a plan.

In February 2011, the planning process culminated with the launch of the Seattle University Youth Initiative, which is housed in the Center for Community Engagement. Through the Youth Initiative the university partners with the city of Seattle, the Seattle Housing Authority, Seattle Public Schools, dozens of community-based organizations, and hundreds of local residents to create a "cradle-to-career" pathway of support for 1,000 children and their families living in a 2-square-mile neighborhood immediately adjacent to campus. In mobilizing the campus to engage, the initiative also deepens the educational experiences of Seattle University students and enhances professional development opportunities for faculty and staff.

The Youth Initiative geographic zone consists of 100 square blocks south of campus that encompass all or a portion of 3 distinct neighborhoods: the Chinatown-International District, Yesler Terrace, and the Central District (see Figure 3.4). These neighborhoods were historically redlined areas due to the Chinese Exclusion Acts, Japanese exclusion and World War II incarceration, and African American segregation, but they nonetheless grew into vibrant cultural communities (Henderson, 2016; Takaki, 1993). The neighborhoods include Seattle's historic and current cultural home of the African American, Chinese American, Filipino American, Japanese American, and Vietnamese

Figure 3.4. Seattle University Youth Initiative.

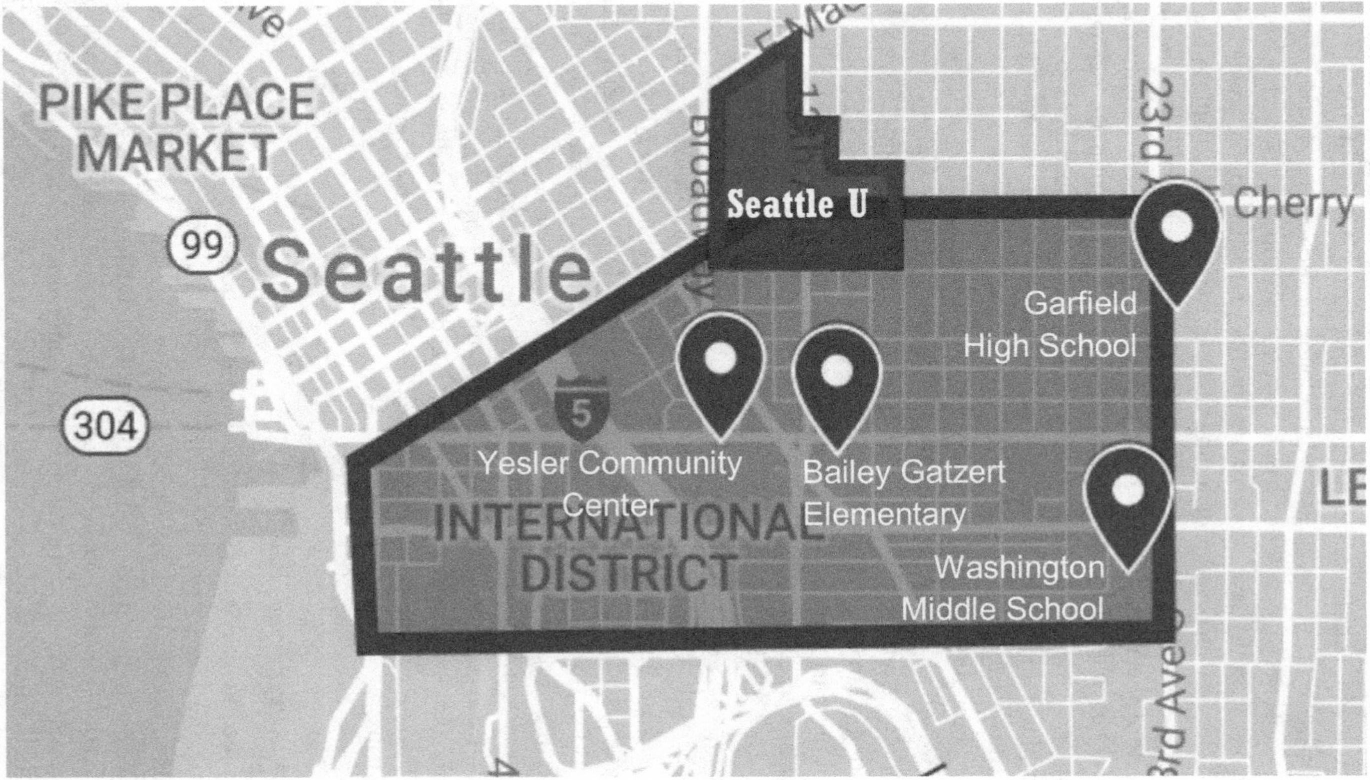

Source. Seattle University. Used with permission.

American communities. In recent years, refugees and immigrants from East Africa and Central America have also moved into the neighborhood.

Over 80% of the 20,000 people living in the neighborhood are renters, and 1 of every 3 residents lives in poverty (Patton, 2012). Youth Initiative partner schools have some of the highest rates of children experiencing homelessness in Seattle, including 20% of the children attending the local elementary school, Bailey Gatzert. Although facing challenges, the neighborhoods of the Youth Initiative also possess incredible assets, including a long history of resident-led advocacy and organizing. In addition, the rich cultural and racial diversity among residents leads to creative approaches to engaging complex issues and a strong sense of community that is not found in many Seattle neighborhoods.

Through the Youth Initiative, the university partners with local schools by providing an extended learning program at Bailey Gatzert Elementary School; organizing a mentoring program at Washington Middle School; and hosting a small alternative high school, Middle College High School, on the university campus. The university also partners with local social services agencies, small businesses, and health-care facilities.

One of the more significant Seattle University Youth Initiative partnerships is with the Seattle Housing Authority. The Housing Authority is currently redeveloping Yesler Terrace, a public housing community located in the middle of the Youth Initiative zone. In 2011 and 2012, the Department of Housing and Urban Development granted the Seattle Housing Authority two Choice Neighborhood grants totaling $30 million to initiate the redevelopment of Yesler Terrace. Seattle University serves as the lead education partner on the Choice Neighborhood project. This has included facilitating a coalition of 5 organizations committed to improving education outcomes for Yesler youth and advising the distribution of almost $3 million of Choice funding for additional education programs for Yesler students.

The University of San Diego

Founded in 1949 as a college for women by the Society of the Sacred Heart, today the University of San Diego is a Catholic coeducational university with an enrollment of over 8,500 students in 43 baccalaureate programs and 37 graduate programs (U.S. Department of Education National Center for Education Statistics, n.d.). The university's mission reflects its Catholic heritage and desire to serve others: "The University of San Diego is a Roman Catholic institution committed to advancing academic excellence, expanding liberal and professional knowledge, creating a diverse and inclusive community and preparing leaders who are dedicated to ethical conduct and compassionate service" (University of San Diego, n.d.).

In the late 1980s, the University of San Diego began developing community engagement partnerships with local organizations. In 1994, with support from a Learn and Serve grant from the Corporation for National and Community Service, University of San Diego faculty began to integrate service into courses through campus-community partnerships. In the ensuing years, staff from the university's Mulvaney Center for Community Awareness and Social Action focused service-learning partnerships on the Linda Vista neighborhood, a community just east of the campus. In addition, several faculty members served in leadership roles at the center in order to develop faculty capacity with engaged scholarship and service-learning in the Linda Vista neighborhood. Thus, in a very organic manner, the University of San Diego developed a place-based community engagement focus in Linda Vista (see Figure 3.5).

In 2015, James T. Harris III was appointed president of the University of San Diego. With a strong background in community engagement, President Harris has centralized community engagement as a strategic platform for the entire university. President Harris's appointment and subsequent efforts to significantly expand and deepen community engagement throughout the university has led to numerous additional campus-community partnerships in the Linda Vista neighborhood.

With a population of approximately 23,000 people, the Linda Vista community is located on the eastern edge of the University of San Diego (Statistical Atlas, n.d.). Linda Vista, Spanish for "beautiful view," is primarily a residential working-class neighborhood with modest ranch-style homes (City of San Diego, n.d.). Originally developed to house aircraft workers during World War II, the community is now home to many immigrants from Mexico, Central America, Africa, and Southeast Asia. Linda Vista is a food desert with only one large ethnic grocery store serving the entire community.

For many years, the Bayside Community Center has served as a primary partner in the University of San Diego's place-based community engagement initiative. The university has partnered with Bayside to enhance neighborhood residents' access to fresh and healthy food by developing a community garden and farmers' market. The university has also supported Bayside's after-school programs by providing university student tutors and mentors. In addition to Bayside, the University of San Diego has numerous partnerships with the San Diego Unified School District in Linda Vista, including Carson Elementary School, Twain Alternative School, and Montgomery Middle School. At Montgomery Middle School, university graduate students in counseling help operate the school's counseling program,

Figure 3.5. University of San Diego, Linda Vista neighborhood.

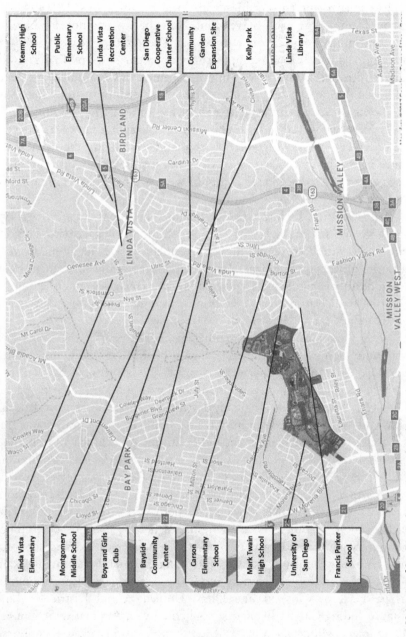

providing valuable social and emotional supports to students. The local Boys and Girls Club and library have also partnered with the university. Finally, the university participates in the Linda Vista Collaborative, which brings together neighborhood leaders for monthly meetings that focus on community and economic development.

Exploration, Development, and Sustaining: Drawing Upon the Initiatives

Much can be gleaned from an in-depth exploration of the history and experiences of these five place-based initiatives. In the next three chapters we will draw upon examples from these institutions to explore lessons learned and promising practices arising from the three distinct phases of mature place-based community engagement efforts.

PART TWO

PHASES OF PLACE-BASED COMMUNITY ENGAGEMENT

4

THE EXPLORATION PHASE

Listening and Visioning

The process of creating a place-based initiative can move quickly or be quite lengthy. Regardless of the time it takes, every institution's approach is often quite distinct. Two central questions frequently guide the exploration phase of a place-based community engagement initiative: (a) Should the institution take on a university-wide community engagement initiative? (b) And if the university decides to pursue an initiative, what shape and form should it take?

During the exploration phase, all five of the institutions we examined in developing this book made a decision to pursue a place-based initiative (see Table 4.1). After investigating its specific context and opportunities, each institution proposed a particular structure and vision for its proposed initiatives. Yet, although they explored the same questions, differences in institutional circumstances, leadership, and community contexts led to a wide variance in how each institution engaged these questions. Drawing upon the five institutional sites, this chapter will explore some of the common characteristics and considerations of the exploration phase of a place-based community engagement initiative, as listed in the following:

- Catalyst(s) for place-based community engagement
- Executive leadership
- Engaging campus and community in a planning process
- Geographic considerations in exploring and identifying the "place"
- Organizational structures and personnel

This chapter concludes with several overall lessons derived from the exploration phase.

TABLE 4.1

Place-Based Community Engagement: Exploration Phase

	Approach to Exploration Phase	Start of Exploration Phase	End of Exploration Phase
Drexel University	Immediate	**2010** President Fry begins his presidency and outlines goal for community engagement in inaugural speech.	
Loyola University Maryland	Formal	**2007** "Year of the City" listening sessions begin.	**2008** "Year of the City" ends.
San Diego State University	Immediate	**1997** Sol Price convenes a meeting to discuss collaborative opportunities in City Heights. At the end of the meeting, President Weber begins partnership work.	
Seattle University	Formal	**2007** Planning period begins.	**2010** Planning period ends.
University of San Diego	Organic	**1980s** Community partnerships develop.	

Catalysts for Place-Based Community Engagement

Place-based community engagement initiatives rarely arise spontaneously. Often one or more catalyzing events or issues spark the institution to respond in new and creative ways. Each of the five institutions we examined experienced a catalyst related to racial and economic injustice that led them to start exploring the possibility of pursuing a place-based initiative.

Safety, Crime, and Demographic Change

A desire to actively address crime and safety issues provided a catalyst for Drexel University, Loyola University Maryland, San Diego State University, and the University of San Diego. In addition to other factors, high rates of crime in dense urban neighborhoods adjacent to their universities led Loyola Maryland in Baltimore and Drexel University in Philadelphia to think more expansively and take action. A demographic change with the rapid influx of

Latina/o and Southeast Asian refugees coupled with high rates of crime and violence in the Linda Vista and City Heights neighborhoods (Price, 2012) near their campuses led the University of San Diego and San Diego State University to pursue ways to support these new residents.

Significant Justice Event/Initiative

Seattle University and Loyola Maryland, both Jesuit Catholic institutions, had additional catalysts arising from the Jesuit imperative "the faith that does justice" (Kolvenbach, 2000). In February 2005, Seattle University hosted a tent city on its campus. For 30 days, Tent City, a publicly sanctioned and resident-led homeless encampment of 100 people, resided on the university's tennis courts. In his campus message announcing that Seattle University would host Tent City, President Stephen Sundborg explained:

> Hosting and offering help to this group of homeless men and women is the right thing for Seattle University to do on many levels—from our Jesuit Catholic focus on service and our practical ability to offer a secure, well-situated venue without disruption to our students and neighbors, to our ability to create meaningful learning and service opportunities for students, faculty, and staff. (S. Sundborg, campus-wide e-mail, November 1, 2004)

Hosting Tent City at Seattle University provided significant community engagement experiences for Seattle University faculty, staff, and students. In addition, residents of Tent City educated the university community about the crisis of homelessness through presentations in courses, public talks, and informal conversations at the encampment. In partnering with Tent City, Seattle University entered uncharted territory. As the first university in the nation to host a homeless encampment, the institution faced new and important questions about what it meant to put its mission and values into practice. The experience also sparked a sense of what might be possible when the entire university focuses on one community engagement effort, planting the idea for what would, years later, become the Seattle University Youth Initiative.

In his inaugural presidential address at Loyola Maryland, the Reverend Brian Linnane challenged the university to become more connected to the city of Baltimore. The following year, Loyola Maryland pursued a "Year of the City" initiative whereby students, faculty, and staff engaged in programs, events, and explorations about Baltimore to "celebrate the city's history and to consider the role Loyola [Maryland], as a Catholic, Jesuit institution of higher learning, should play in addressing the challenges faced by the City" ("Year of the City Sets the Tone for 2006–2007," 2008).

Through the "Year of the City," the entire campus had an opportunity to experience the beauty of the region as well as better understand its challenges, including major economic disparities, lack of quality housing, and educational inequities, all arising from systemic racism and lack of economic development by the city and state. Through numerous community encounters faculty, staff, and students experienced the divide between the low-income African American community residing in neighborhoods adjacent to campus and the wealthier and predominantly White Loyola Maryland community. These experiences led to a call to action with a recognition that Loyola Maryland needed to respond to the systemic justice issues in its wider community.

Presidential Transition

At two institutions, Drexel and the University of San Diego, the beginning of a new presidency also served as a key catalyst for pursuing place-based community engagement. The next section will provide more details on the role of university leadership in promoting a place-based approach.

Executive Leadership

Although not required at this phase, executive leadership, whether on the university campus or from major financial contributors, often plays an important role in initiating place-based community engagement efforts. All five of the institutions we examine in this book had significant presidential involvement. In most cases, the university president initiated the exploration of a place-based initiative. In addition, for two institutions, San Diego State University and Seattle University, a major financial supporter from the business community also played a major role.

For Drexel and the University of San Diego, the selection of a new president who had significant experience with community engagement prior to appointment led to a major university-wide emphasis on place-based community engagement. When John Fry became the president of Drexel in 2010, he challenged Drexel to become "the most civically engaged campus in the country" (Drexel University Office of University and Community Partnerships, n.d.a), with a significant emphasis on partnerships in its local neighborhood. In 2015, James T. Harris III became president of the University of San Diego and immediately began engaging the university and its neighbors in efforts to considerably expand partnerships.

In examining the backgrounds of these two presidents, three key points emerge. First, both are seasoned presidents; Drexel is the second presidency for Fry, and the University of San Diego is Harris's third presidency. Second, both presidents are well known in the field for community engagement. Prior to his first presidency, Fry led a nationally recognized coalition of campus and community partners to redevelop Philadelphia's University City neighborhood through his role as executive vice president at the University of Pennsylvania (Drexel University Office of the President, n.d.). Harris published an article (Harris & Pickron-Davis, 2013) highlighting his work with community engagement at Widener University and has also served on the national Campus Compact board, a national coalition of 1,200 college and university presidents dedicated to promoting civic engagement among college students.

Third, both presidents had successfully utilized community engagement as a central strategy at their prior institutions. For example, before his appointment at Drexel, Fry served as president for 8 years at Franklin and Marshall College, where he led an intensive effort to strengthen campus-community partnerships with the City of Lancaster and local organizations (Snyder, 2016). During his 13 years as president at Widener University, Harris established a consortium which eventually developed a College Access Center serving all of Delaware County, Pennsylvania (Harris & Pickron-Davis, 2013). Harris also opened a university-based charter school, and the university has received recognition on the President's Higher Education Community Service Honor Roll each year since 2006.

At San Diego State University and Seattle University, two major local business leaders provided initial financial resources that helped both institutions gain momentum in their pursuit of place-based community engagement. Jim Sinegal, cofounder of Costco, contributed funds for a planning process and quietly advocated for Seattle University to increase its commitment to the local neighborhood (Sinegal, 2015). Sol Price, president of Price Philanthropies, sought out San Diego State University as a major partner in his substantial effort to improve the City Heights neighborhood of San Diego (Price, 2012). Sinegal and Price's encouragement and financial support significantly strengthened the resolve of Seattle University and San Diego State University's leadership to pursue place-based work. The involvement of Sinegal and Price also demonstrates the potential for place-based strategies to engage major business and philanthropic leaders in new and more expansive ways.

Engaging Campus and Community: The Planning Process

During the exploration phase the five campuses pursued three distinct approaches to planning: formal, organic, and/or immediate. These engagement or planning strategies were highly contingent on the campus culture and the role of the president.

Planning Process

Formal

Seattle University and Loyola Maryland engaged in formal planning processes reflecting their campus cultures. Prior to launching the Youth Initiative, Seattle University spent 3 years engaging with the campus and community, including multiple focus groups, community meetings, and a conference that brought together 300 campus and community leaders to offer guidance and advice on the development of the initiative. John McKay, a former federal attorney and faculty member in the School of Law, led a formal yearlong campus committee that conducted thorough research and outreach on a variety of topics. Seattle University's outreach and engagement process culminated in the creation and presentation of a strategic plan that the university's board of trustees approved in November 2010. During this lengthy planning process, Seattle University convened an informal advisory board or "kitchen cabinet" to guide strategy. This important practice led naturally to the development of a more formal advisory board during the development phase of the initiative.

Driven by a desire to fully understand and engage the root causes of the crime and safety issues of its local neighborhoods, Loyola Maryland pursued a two-year planning process to develop the York Road Initiative. After the "Year of the City," Loyola Maryland's community and government relations office led an additional yearlong listening project to better understand the needs and concerns of the wider community in order to inform additional university and community actions. Faculty, staff, and students engaged in service projects and attended events to learn more about the city of Baltimore. There were also many community meetings where organizations and residents were able to voice their perspectives on many issues, including how they might best be engaged with the university. The leadership of Loyola Maryland's community and government relations office is noteworthy as the other four institutions organized their initiatives from their community engagement and/or academic affairs divisions.

Organic

The University of San Diego has a campus culture of intensive collaboration and the organic development of ideas and university initiatives. Reflecting this dynamic, the university's place-based initiative grew gradually from the work of a small group of faculty and the Center for Community Service-Learning, which later became the Mulvaney Center for Community, Awareness and Social Action.

Several senior faculty members began place-based work long before it became a university-wide strategy. The current faculty liaison for the center, also a professor of sociology, noted that her practice of connecting her courses and research to the community has long focused on the Linda Vista neighborhood. She observed that over a period of many years, her community engagement practice, along with the practice of several of her faculty colleagues, shifted from a problem-based to an asset-based approach. She described this shift as "Not for you but with you." Reflecting on the success of this asset-based approach, the current codirector of the Impact Linda Vista Initiative (an associate professor of Spanish) noted, "We get invited to community conversations because they want us there." In many ways, this slow and steady development of a core group of faculty practitioners established a foundation for the university to pursue a more expansive focus on place-based engagement.

At the same time that this small group of faculty was deepening and expanding involvement, the Center for Community Service-Learning was developing partnerships for students to consistently engage in voluntary service and academic service-learning in the Linda Vista neighborhood. Beginning in the late 1980s and continuing over many academic years, center staff, specifically the director, cultivated strong relationships with Linda Vista community leaders, enabling the development of long-term and intensive partnerships. Thus, for the University of San Diego, the movement toward the development phase was neither formal nor immediate; the commitment to place-based partnerships in Linda Vista grew steadily through the natural evolution of faculty and staff involvement over almost two decades.

Immediate

A sense of urgency from their university presidents guided the planning process for Drexel and San Diego State University. As noted earlier, President Fry of Drexel and President Harris of the University of San Diego use community engagement as a central platform for the entire university and have played major roles in starting the process of exploration at their institutions. President Fry (2010) used his inaugural convocation speech to declare, "Let us mark today as the beginning of a new phase of a high-impact university-community partnership that will lift Drexel University and its surrounding neighborhoods to new heights." Presenting his strategic vision that centers community engagement as a driver of Drexel's continued growth and evolution, Fry (2010) stated, "The future of Drexel and our community are inextricably bound, in a mutual self-interest that virtually dictates our support for one another."

When he arrived at the University of San Diego in 2015, President Harris brought with him a strong commitment to place-based engagement. In his first academic convocation, Harris (2016) noted, "We are about engaging the local community in meaningful ways that brings about positive change in society." Describing how this might take place, Harris (2016) stated, "We will continue to seek to develop a culture of engagement—on campus and off—in students, alumni and the [University of San Diego] community to be engaged with the university and to serve the greater good . . . [and] to remain mindful that we have certain assets and resources and to be the best possible stewards of those resources."

For the University of San Diego, President Harris's leadership and sense of urgency enabled the university and its community partners to quickly build on the place-based focus that had organically developed since the late 1980s. In essence, President Harris sparked a second cycle of exploration, development, and sustaining to build off the long history of the university's focus on its local community, particularly the Linda Vista neighborhood. Although different from Drexel, the example of presidential leadership at the University of San Diego demonstrates that a new presidency can reset the clock and energy for a place-based strategy. For the University of San Diego, President Harris's leadership will likely take the initiative to new prominence.

In 1996, Stephen Weber became president of San Diego State University. Shortly after his arrival, Sol Price, a well-known San Diego business leader and philanthropist, approached Weber requesting San Diego State University's involvement in supporting the community of City Heights, a neighborhood adjacent to San Diego State University's campus. Weber quickly responded by engaging various academic leaders in working with Price, along with leaders from the city of San Diego and San Diego Unified School District, to form creative and expansive new partnerships in City Heights (Price, 2012). During Weber's 15-year tenure, his commitment and direct involvement, including frequent meetings with Price, led to a rapid growth in the university's involvement in City Heights. San Diego State University, led by now President Emeritus Weber, provides an example of how a university can quickly move through a planning process in order to immediately respond to community needs and opportunities through a comprehensive focus on place-based community engagement.

Geographic Considerations: Identifying and Exploring Place

In exploring a geographically focused initiative, campuses often have many factors to consider, including the proximity of the "place" to the campus, community needs and assets, existing partnerships, and the desires of donors and other influential leaders. Three distinct themes emerged from the institutions we examined. First, several institutions chose to concentrate on geographic areas in close proximity to the university experiencing significant issues of inequity and injustice. Second, although proximity to campus was important, for two additional institutions, partnering with an existing community collaborative provided the key factor in selecting where to focus. Third, for one institution, the invitation and advocacy of a donor led to the emphasis on a particular geographic area.

Proximity, Needs, and Assets

Drexel and Seattle University chose their geographic focus based on the proximity of the neighborhood to their campus and the community's needs and assets. Recognizing that its success was intricately connected to the success of its neighbors, Drexel chose to concentrate on the neighborhoods of Mantua and Powelton Village, two communities immediately adjacent to the university. In developing the initiative, Drexel's senior vice provost of university and community partnerships went to neighborhood leaders and shared Drexel's desire to deepen and expand its partnerships. She noted, "Our approach was to go to the community and ask if Drexel could be included in their planning initiatives." This method built on the assets of the community and avoided the potential pitfall of the university imposing its vision or its plan on the community.

Like Drexel, Seattle University also chose to partner with neighborhoods adjacent to its campus. This choice arose after a lengthy process of examining community needs and assets, mapping existing campus-community partnerships, and factoring in practical considerations like the ability of university students to get to community organizations and the attendance zone for local schools. During its planning process, the university noted that its local neighborhoods faced major challenges, with many residents experiencing significant economic and educational inequities. The university also noted that neighborhood residents and local organizations held tremendous assets in community leadership, a history of advocacy, and an ability to engage across cultural and racial differences. This recognition led naturally to Seattle University opting to pursue a long-term place-based strategy in its immediate neighborhoods. The university confirmed the final boundaries of its Youth Initiative when, in 2010, Seattle Public Schools set up a new neighborhood attendance zone for Bailey Gatzert Elementary School encompassing an area of 100 square blocks just south of the university.

Existing Collaboratives

Loyola Maryland and the University of San Diego drew upon their relationships with existing neighborhood collaboratives to determine the geographic parameters of their respective place-based initiatives. For Loyola Maryland, the existence of the York Road commercial corridor working group and the nonprofit organization the York Road Collaborative, both groups that it was already involved with, led naturally to a focus on York Road. Although not the deciding factor, York Road is also conveniently located on the eastern edge of the Loyola Maryland campus.

The University of San Diego had long partnered with the Linda Vista Collaborative, which unites nonprofit organizations, schools, and religious organizations to better serve the Linda Vista community. Hundreds of university students had served in Linda Vista collaborative organizations, and numerous university faculty and staff had developed strong working relationships with many collaborative members. In addition, several University of San Diego faculty and staff frequently participated in the collaborative's meetings, contributing to overall neighborhood cohesion and strategy. Thus, for the University of San Diego, centering place-based efforts on the Linda Vista community would be a natural outgrowth of the work that it was already performing via the collaborative.

Donor Driven

At some institutions, a persuasive donor may significantly influence the selection of the place-based geography. For San Diego State University, Price Philanthropies and Sol Price's personal commitment to support City Heights residents and improve the community had a substantial impact on determining its geographic parameters. Sol Price's prodigious ability to convene city and school officials and his commitment of financial resources to support San Diego State University's involvement led the university to quickly adopt the City Heights neighborhood and focus on educational partnerships (Price, 2012). As President Emeritus Weber reflected, "One of the spokes of the wheel was education; [Sol Price] called me over because he thought [San Diego State University] should be interested. I had not been with someone who had that change agenda, and I was excited right away."

Organizational Structures and Personnel: Internal Assessment and Action

Prior to engaging in university-wide place-based initiatives, institutions assess their current organizational structures and personnel. All of the institutions we examined utilized this important strategy, yet each institution pursued a different organizational tactic and structure to guide its exploration phase.

Cabinet Level

Often in higher education, cabinet-level leadership guides major institutional change and controls budgeting, which can contribute significantly to the success of university-wide initiatives. Positioning leaders at the highest levels of the university to guide its place-based approach demonstrated the value each of these institutions placed on the importance of its initiative and the commitment to success. At Drexel, San Diego State University, and during the second rendition of place-based work at the University of San Diego, a designated cabinet-level administrator provided leadership of the institution's place-based strategy. Drexel created a position of senior vice provost to lead its endeavor, at San Diego State University the president directly led the initiative, and the University of San Diego (most recently) appointed an assistant provost to guide strategy and partnerships for its effort.

Director Level

In some cases, there was not a cabinet-level administrator leading the place-based initiative. At Loyola Maryland and Seattle University, their initiatives' highest administrator during the exploration phase served at the director's level. At Seattle University, the director of the Center for Community Engagement, serving in a temporary role as special assistant to the provost, led the exploration phase. Loyola Maryland created a position of director of the York Road Initiative who reported to the vice president for administration. A key difference between the leader of a place-based initiative serving at the director versus cabinet level is that typically an intermediary (provost, vice provost, or vice president) represents the initiative at the cabinet level. This can be helpful if the intermediary is a strong advocate (e.g., at Loyola Maryland and Seattle University) but a challenge if the intermediary is less supportive.

Lessons Learned From the Exploration Phase

As described throughout this chapter, the exploration phase of a place-based community engagement initiative frequently brings a sense of excitement and promise. It also calls on institutions to think strategically and purposefully. Five central lessons arise from the exploration phase:

1. *Follow the energy of the catalyst.* Most institutions pursuing place-based community engagement experience an initial spark or catalyst that moves them to action. The catalyzing event or dynamic will vary significantly from campus to campus. Recognizing the catalyst and drawing upon its energy can ignite the exploration phase.
2. *Presidential leadership and donor support matters.* Although not essential, the leadership of the university president and investment from one or more financial supporters can significantly strengthen the prospects of an institution's place-based community engagement strategy.
3. *There is no blueprint for the planning process.* An institution that values more formal processes will take more time in planning, whereas institutions led by a president with significant community engagement experience may move rapidly. Still other institutions may organically develop their strategies and commitment over many years. The fact that there is not a script to developing a plan can prove challenging but ultimately provides the freedom to develop an initiative that reflects the context of each community and campus.
4. *Go where you already have partners.* In general, selecting a "place" to engage based upon strong existing campus and community partners will significantly increase the potential for success. Focusing on community assets and not just on a community's needs or deficits also improves the potential for long-term results.
5. *Invest in the leadership of the initiative.* Institutions that appoint a senior-level and/or seasoned administrator to develop the initiative boost their possibilities for success.

By drawing upon these lessons and the observations we have presented in this chapter, universities and their communities can position themselves for a successful launch of a place-based community engagement initiative. The next chapter explores key elements for developing an initiative.

5

THE DEVELOPMENT PHASE

Experimenting and Growing

O nce an institution decides to pursue a place-based initiative, the fast-paced development phase begins (see Table 5.1). During this phase, partnerships and programs move through a period of rapid experimentation, with the beginning of new activities and modifications to existing efforts. During the development phase, university leadership focuses on increasing funding and other resources for the initiative, frequently by pursuing external nonuniversity funding. Organizational structures and staffing also begin to change, including the reorganization of existing offices and, in some cases, the creation of entirely new divisions. A central indicator of success for this phase is if/when awareness of the initiative saturates the university and its wider communities, providing the momentum to move toward sustainability.

Partnerships and Programs: Experimentation

During the development phase, all the institutions we studied experimented with new partnerships and programs and modified many of their existing efforts. The executive director of Seattle University's initiative and Drexel's executive director for neighborhood partnerships both described this process as "throwing spaghetti on the wall and seeing what sticks."

Key Partners for Place-Based Engagement

Developing a handful of key community partners is a central component of place-based community engagement and this was true for all five of the institutions we studied. Drexel and Loyola Maryland have major city and government partnerships. Seattle University's and San Diego State

TABLE 5.1

Place-Based Community Engagement: Development Phase

	Start of Development Phase	End of Development Phase	Initiative Director(s)	Cabinet-Level Initiative Representative
Drexel University	**2010** Hiring of vice provost for university and community partnerships	**2014** Dornsife Center opened and receives U.S. Housing and Urban Development "Promise Zone" grant	Vice provost for university and community partnerships	President
Loyola University Maryland	**2008** End of "Year of the City"	**2016** Merger of York Road Initiative and Center for Community Service and Justice	Director, Center for Community Service and Justice	Vice president for administration
San Diego State University	**1997** After meeting with Sol Price to discuss collaborative opportunities in City Heights	**2011** Retirement of President Weber from San Diego State University	*Internally Facing:* Vice provost and dean of the College of Education *Externally Facing:* President	President
Seattle University	**2011** Postplanning; becomes lead education partner in Seattle Housing Authority's U.S. Housing and Urban Development Choice Neighborhood grant	**2015** Center name change and staff reorganization	Executive director, Center for Community Engagement	Associate provost
University of San Diego	**1980s** Community partnership development	**2009** Hiring of externally facing director	Director, Mulvaney Center for Community, Awareness and Social Action	Provost

University's main partners are schools and school districts. The University of San Diego has a unique key partner, the Bayside Community Center, whose development mirrors the university's organic initiative development. Although in this phase each institution had major partnerships that focused on specific topics, they also had secondary partnerships spanning many issues and sectors.

Community and Governmental Partners
The leadership of Drexel and Loyola Maryland's initiatives have extensive community and government relations experiences, including in the geographic areas of their respective efforts. The senior vice provost for university and community partnerships, who leads Drexel's initiative, had extensive prior experiences working in university and community relations in Philadelphia. At Loyola Maryland, the vice president for administration played a critical role in developing the York Road Initiative. The backgrounds and institutional roles of both of these leaders naturally led to the development of strong city and government partnerships.

Drexel's initiative included a strong emphasis on the connection between economic and housing development. In particular, Philadelphia's Local Initiatives Support Coalition (LISC), the local office of the largest community development organization in the United States, served as a key partner and facilitated a planning process for Drexel's engagement. The senior vice provost shared, "We met as a broad collaborative, with LISC and a number of community partners, every month for several years and that led to an application for the federal Promise Zone designation in 2013/2014." Drexel's partnership with LISC and the many community, city, government, and other nonprofit partners in their Promise Zone and their subsequent successful Promise Neighborhood implementation grant served as a major component of their partnership portfolio in the West Philadelphia neighborhoods of Mantua and Powelton Village.

At Loyola Maryland, the vice president had a background in government and community relations. The director of the York Road Initiative also had extensive community relations experiences, most recently leading a nonprofit that worked with the city of Baltimore and community leaders. The director's strong professional relationships with elected officials contributed significantly to Loyola's success in developing its initiative. For example, the director frequently attended city council meetings and one city council member, in particular, often sought her advice on the city's agenda and policies. Because of these strong relationships and shared experiences, Loyola Maryland's decision to focus on the York Road area coincided directly with the city's commercial corridor development as well as York Road's close proximity to the university.

Education and School Partners

P–12 schools, particularly those located in urban settings, face significant challenges including a culture of frequent and mandated assessment, high staff turnover, and the complexities of offering culturally relevant curricula to racially and linguistically diverse student populations. With a primary focus on education equity, San Diego State University and Seattle University worked through the complexity of these challenges to develop strong reciprocal school partnerships that would lead to greater educational equity for children and families.

San Diego State University chose to focus its education partnerships on a feeder pattern of three San Diego Unified School District schools (an elementary school, a middle school, and a high school) in San Diego's City Heights neighborhood. Through the encouragement of Sol Price of Price Philanthropies, in 1997 San Diego State University's president met with school district leaders to establish the partnership. Shortly after the creation of the partnership, San Diego State University appointed a new dean of their College of Education who had previously served as a superintendent of a diverse urban school district in New York, had been the commissioner of education in Texas, and came with strong community engagement experiences.

The partnership between San Diego State University and the San Diego Unified School District began by focusing on Rosa Parks Elementary School. At that time, Rosa Parks Elementary was underperforming and struggling to attract students and families. San Diego State University's President Emeritus Weber explained, "It was a school where the savvy parents transferred their children to other higher performing and affluent schools." With the leadership and funding of Price Philanthropies and the expertise of San Diego State University faculty, Rosa Parks Elementary teachers were provided with strong professional development and resources to develop innovative curricula to more fully address the needs of their students. Within a short time, the educational performance of students increased significantly and the school became a first choice for families—so much so that it became overcrowded.

One particular program, School in the Park, illustrates the unique entrepreneurial spirit of the Price, San Diego State University, and San Diego Unified School District partnership. As Rosa Parks Elementary exceeded its capacity, "bungalows," temporary structures that resemble shipping containers, were brought to the campus. Noting that these classroom spaces were not conducive to a good student learning environment, Price Philanthropies devised an idea of taking Rosa Parks Elementary students to local museums to supplement their learning and mitigate the issue of lack of classroom space. San Diego State University's College of Education faculty worked with the school district to develop a flexible field-based curriculum. In lieu of attending class in the bungalows, students went to museums and had their "school in the park"—literally learning their lessons by rotating through city and regional museums.

After its initial success at Rosa Parks Elementary, the San Diego State University, San Diego Unified School District, and Price Philanthropies partnership expanded to middle school and high school. The partnership has become the "College Avenue Compact," a comprehensive P–20 college preparatory program encompassing Rosa Parks Elementary School, Clark Monroe Middle School, and Hoover High School. During the development phase, the "College Avenue Compact" provided college advising and ultimately an opportunity to matriculate to San Diego State University on a full four-year tuition scholarship. Once at San Diego State University, "College Avenue Compact" students have an opportunity to become paid mentors at the City Heights schools they attended.

Like San Diego State University, Seattle University worked closely with its local school district, Seattle Public Schools, to develop an intensive P–20 partnership focusing on children and families living in the attendance zone of Bailey Gatzert Elementary School (Gatzert). Recognizing the potential risk of expanding too quickly, Seattle University chose to initially concentrate its efforts on developing a community school model with Gatzert. Community schools unite multiple community partners and a school to pursue expansive academic enhancements, health and social services, and family and youth development programming (Institute for Educational Leadership, 2015).

Seattle University's initial partnerships with Gatzert included the development of an after-school program for Gatzert students. The program provides one-to-one academic support and enrichment activities such as filmmaking, an engineering club, a running program, and a dance class. In addition to the after-school program, Seattle University placed math tutors in Gatzert classrooms through a program called the Seattle University Math Corps (SUM Corps). Family engagement activities were another component, including an English language learner program for non-English-speaking parents and outings to local museums and sports events. The university has also utilized its role as a convener to support the addition of a school clinic and preschool classroom at Gatzert Elementary. Finally, the university has assisted the school with the collection and analysis of data to improve teaching, learning, and the school climate.

In addition to school partnerships, Seattle University also has a major partnership with the local housing authority. As described in chapter 3, in 2011 and 2012, Seattle University partnered on the Seattle Housing Authority's successful attainment of two Choice Neighborhood grants totaling $30 million for the redevelopment of the Yesler Terrace public housing community. Seattle University serves as the lead education partner in the Choice Neighborhood effort. As such, Seattle University facilitates monthly meetings of education partners and also tracks education data through a full-time analyst funded by the grant.

Partnership With Community Centers

Bayside in the Linda Vista neighborhood began as a faith-based one-stop settlement house in the 1930s serving low-income families regardless of immigration status (Bayside Community Center, n.d.). The University of San Diego has a long history of partnering with Bayside that predates the development of the Mulvaney Center. Paralleling the organic nature of the University of San Diego's engagement with the Linda Vista community, the Bayside partnership grew naturally over many years.

The current executive director of the center, an alumnus of the university, places great trust in the university and values the partnership. The director observed that the university-Bayside partnerships include food distribution, front desk organization, garden work, and selling at the farmers' market, as well as a senior lunch program, English as a second language (ESL) classes, and academic clubs at two elementary schools. There is also a Bayside–Nursing School partnership involving offering exercise programs, giving wellness checks, and doing community-based research with the senior population. University of San Diego nursing students and faculty also provide health-related services to Linda Vista residents who gather at Bayside.

One particular university-Bayside partnership established during this phase was a local farmers' market that continues today. The Linda Vista neighborhood is a noted food desert (Healthy Communities Assessment Tool, n.d.). The Bayside program manager, an alumna of the University of San Diego, partnered with the university to develop the farmers' market. The Bayside Community Center, with assistance from university students, also grew produce to sell at the market that continues to serve a multigenerational and diverse community.

(Re)Developing Curricula and Programs

During the development of their place-based initiative, all of the institutions we studied went through a process of developing or redeveloping curricula and programs. Noting the need to expand to a university-wide approach, the institutions used a number of strategies to change and develop curricular programs.

Service-Learning and Community-Based Research
Service-learning and community-based research are the most common forms of curricular-based community engagement on college campuses (Astin, Vogelgesang, Ikeda, & Yee, 2000; Eyler & Giles, 1999). In developing their place-based initiative all five institutions reexamined existing service-learning and community-based research opportunities throughout the university. For example, Loyola Maryland shifted their curricular emphasis from a focus on charity work toward a transformational model accentuating justice. Reflecting on this shift, the York Road initiative director commented:

> The luxury of having a place-based [initiative] is building a continuum with the community. We are constantly being able to grow and add [partnerships and programs]. For example, it is harder when some of our long-term programs, a meal program at a faith-based institution, [are] a charity program[s], and it is not possible to develop further.

With a transformational model, it is possible to maintain long-standing partnerships while pursuing new programs and partnerships. Such a model acknowledges that charity and justice are both needed and can occur simultaneously.

Clinical and Internship Programs
Internships and clinical work were also important curricular opportunities that engaged students, particularly graduate students, in professional preparation programs. Through their place-based approach, three campuses offered strong clinical opportunities.

Drexel University is well known for its cooperative learning model in which students take "breaks" from their courses on campus to do paid and unpaid apprenticeship experiences that enhance their education. For example, an alum of Drexel partnered with Co-op students to open a coffee shop on campus, the only student-run coffeehouse in the country (Drexel University, n.d.b). During the development phase, many Drexel students chose to do their Co-op experience with organizations in the Mantua and Powelton Village neighborhoods.

Located on York Road, the Loyola Maryland Clinical Centers serve as an off-the-main-campus university laboratory for graduate and undergraduate student clinical experiences in a variety of educational, health, and mental health areas, including audiology, literacy, mental and pastoral counseling,

psychological services, and speech-language pathology. During the development phase, faculty researchers worked on-site, which allowed for meaningful community-based research. The state-of-the-art facility also provided
computer labs and storage for students who were doing their clinical experiences as well as space for community events.

During the development phase, with support from Price Philanthropies,
San Diego State University provided clinical and internship experiences to
students in the College of Education and School of Social Work to address
the educational and social needs of students and families in City Heights
schools. Through paid internships, School of Social Work students, many of
whom were from City Heights or neighborhoods like City Heights, provided
counseling support to neighborhood children and parents. In the College
of Education, student teachers had an opportunity to complete internship
hours at Rosa Parks Elementary School, Monroe Middle School, or Hoover
High School.

Building Faculty Capacity
Two institutions in our study utilized creative, although quite different,
strategies to build faculty capacity. Seattle University created a $50,000
Fund for Engagement, inviting faculty and staff to pursue creative ideas to
engage in the Youth Initiative. Not a typical request for proposals, applicants
could submit ideas to create a new program, enhance curriculum, develop
a community-based research project, or mobilize student clubs and organizations. During a 2-year period, faculty and staff submitted 50 proposals,
with 20 projects receiving funding. Fund for Engagement projects included
a college visit program organized by faculty from the College of Education,
a citizenship class sponsored by the School of Law, and a summer robotics
program organized by the College of Science and Engineering.

The shift from a charity to a transformational model enabled Loyola
Maryland to build faculty capacity and reach faculty who had not been
previously connected to the university-wide strategy. A long-standing
justice-focused faculty member, who had not been previously involved with
the Center for Community Service and Justice, was recruited to support
faculty service-learning and engaged research. The faculty director shared,
"[With our former office and its charity-centered model], I didn't even see
any connections between my work and the job description (faculty director). The position was not connected to my interests in Baltimore which
are racial and justice issues." A shift to a more expansive place-based community engagement approach expanded and deepened faculty involvement.
The faculty director noted, "We are now reaching faculty that we have not
reached before." This included faculty members who were already doing

justice-based community work but did not partner with the center as well as new faculty who may be more interested in the justice-oriented approach.

Strong Multicultural and Identity Development
Partnering intensively with communities that have a long history of systemic racial discrimination and economic challenges required attending to multicultural and identity development, especially of university students and staff. Deep and expansive explorations of race, class, gender, and the many other dimensions of multiculturalism and intersecting identities led to stronger connections (and subsequently partnerships) across diverse individuals and organizations. For university and community partnerships, not attending to these topics often causes unnecessary miscommunication and misunderstanding that can erode trust and limit long-term impact. The University of San Diego and San Diego State University had two innovative ways of doing this important work that has been historically ignored or not intentionally addressed by the service-learning field.

Unlike the other institutions in our study, the University of San Diego's staff at the Mulvaney Center for Community, Awareness and Social Action is majority People of Color,[1] with a wide range of races and identities represented, including African American, Asian American, Latina/o, Middle Eastern, multiracial, Pinoy, first-generation college graduates, and veterans of multiple branches of the military. The Mulvaney Center's commitment to diversity went beyond the identities of its staff. During this phase, the center staff placed significant emphasis on multicultural content and deep reflection of diverse identities before students even went out into the community. Reflecting on this practice, the Mulvaney Center associate director shared, "You can address it in training or in resources. Fundamental change starts inside, not outside."

The Mulvaney Center's leadership course that prepares students for service-learning experiences placed a major emphasis on multicultural competency and identity work. For example, two of the courses' learning outcomes included the following:

> *Cultural competency:* (a) Is self-aware of own culture and has better understanding/awareness of personal role in creating social justice and (b) values and respects differences
>
> *Community responsibility:* (a) Identifies personal ability (aptitude, gift) and responsibility to use such abilities in order to serve community locally and at large and (b) participates in service component to provide experiential understanding of the importance of community service and social justice/action

In addition, the key texts for the course included Mitchell's (2008) article on critical service-learning and McIntosh's (1989) widely known article on unpacking White privilege.

Although strong multicultural awareness learning outcomes and content are foundational, the facilitation of this content (and students' application of this learning at their sites) was what brought this material to life. Mulvaney Center staff and their faculty partners who taught this leadership course and conducted other types of training demonstrated a sense of comfort and ease when talking about multicultural content in ways that are not common in most service-learning offices. Conversations we observed among staff and students in the Mulvaney Center and positive feedback from community partners and diverse residents provided more evidence to illustrate the strong multicultural competency of the staff to train students to work in the community.

San Diego State University also attended to multicultural competency and identity development but through an intergenerational social work lens. As noted earlier in this chapter, one of San Diego State University's main partnerships with the San Diego Unified School District was the placement of social workers in elementary schools as part of their clinical experience. With financial support from Price Philanthropies, San Diego State University and the San Diego Unified School District also cosponsored a program for City Heights high school students to learn about social work through exploratory internships. Reflecting on the importance of this program, the director of the social work program shared, "Social work is not necessarily a profession that low-income high school students are aware of. Our program introduces the field and the work as part of a college preparatory curriculum with our partnership with College Avenue Compact."

A true pipeline program, through the social work partnership San Diego State University students from City Heights and communities like City Heights facilitated multicultural competency and identity development for City Heights high school students. As college students shared their own experiences and taught the high school students the disciplinary knowledge learned in college, they provided a new meaning to identity development and multicultural competency. In many ways, the San Diego State University experience represented many of the values and outcomes the University of San Diego leadership course aims to teach, except the focus was on students from City Heights.

Resources and Funding: Increasing Capacity

During the development phase, a significant component of a place-based community engagement initiative is the need to secure additional resources and funding. During this development phase, the level of success in acquiring resources determines the type and scope of innovation that takes place in the short term. In addition, adequately resourcing the initiative during this period of time often influences the depth and breadth of the initiative for years to come. Yet fund development is new territory for most leaders of an initiative and quickly becomes a bigger part of their job than they expected. This is especially true for directors who lead a more traditional office of service-learning prior to their initiative. Much like with programs and partnerships, during this phase bringing in new resources and external funding is also experimental, involving many strategies.

University Resources and Funding

Three of the institutions in our study, Loyola Maryland, Seattle University, and the University of San Diego, did not receive substantial additional university funding during the development phase but creatively drew upon their existing university budget, pursued external funding, and amplified campus partnerships to move their work forward. For example, during this phase Seattle University leveraged the impact of its student employment program by deciding to concentrate all of its community service work-study funding, about 15% of its annual allocation from the federal government, on placing paid students with Youth Initiative partners. Seattle University also invited other campus units to concentrate community programming on the Youth Initiative neighborhood.

Drexel University and San Diego State University had a different internal funding dynamic. At both institutions, the university president had significant influence in resourcing and/or directing funds to the place-based efforts. At Drexel, this was done with both financial and nonfinancial resources. For example, because Drexel utilized community engagement as a major platform of its strategic plan, the university invested significant financial resources into the initiative in the form of new offices and additional staff. Drexel developed an entire new division focused on university and community engagement. In addition, the university created an Office of Corporate Relations and Economic Development that, in large part, also supported place-based community engagement on the campus.

Drexel also established an in-house director of university and community partnerships, an office which concentrated much of its efforts on external grant development. Drexel's unique Home Purchase Assistance Program encouraged and supported home ownership within the parameters of the place-based boundaries. Key components of this program included a $15,000 forgivable loan for new purchases and $5,000 home renovation grants that were also forgivable (Drexel University Human Resources, n.d.).

San Diego State University worked exclusively with Price Philanthropies to fund its expansive new efforts, and the president provided the leadership necessary to get the campus more deeply engaged in the City Heights partnership. San Diego State University's president asked the College of Education and School of Social Work to engage in the City Heights Initiative. Price Philanthropies agreed to support these new San Diego State University activities, which minimized the need to draw upon university funding. For example, the College of Education shifted its teacher preparation and placement practices to partner with City Heights schools. Price Philanthropies provided scholarships or stipends for these graduate students to earn master's degrees in teaching. In this way, the president brought financial support to the university through the partnership, which contributed to the College of Education's enrollment strategy.

External Funding

External funding is essential to attain the ambitious vision of place-based engagement. All of the institutions that we studied sought out external funding, including government and foundation grants and gifts from individuals. Each university's distinct fund development structures and strategies led to different approaches to pursuing additional support. Two major themes arising from the institutions we studied include the role of presidential stewardship (Drexel and San Diego State University) and director stewardship (Loyola Maryland, Seattle University, and the University of San Diego).

Presidential Stewardship

Led by the director of university and community partnerships, Drexel had an in-house team that worked on community engagement–oriented grants. Prior to her appointment to this position, the director had worked as a grant-writer within another Drexel academic unit. Reflecting on her unit's organizational structure the director shared, "It is important that we keep a very lean internal structure—meaning minimal support staff." For Drexel, even with their hundreds of programs and partnerships across the university, only a small number of staff worked on procuring external grants.

At Drexel the positive reputation of President Fry and the senior vice provost for university and community partnerships in the field of community engagement and higher education led to their active role in fund development efforts related to their place-based initiative. For example, in 2012 the president and senior vice provost played a major role in working with the

Dornsife family on a $10 million investment to support Drexel's place-based approach, particularly the new neighborhood extension office that became the Dornsife Center.

San Diego State University's President Weber played a major role in the university's fund development efforts related to the City Heights Initiative. President Weber's strong relationship with Sol Price led Price Philanthropies to ask the university to become one of its two primary education partners. San Diego State University did not solicit Price Philanthropies with a grant request; rather, Price and Weber agreed upon a partnership model, and Price made the financial investments in the innovative practices that emerged.

For the university, being a primary partner with a philanthropic organization that drew upon its business acumen (Sol Price, in creating Price Club, was the founder of the big box store model) also provided unique learning moments. In looking back at this time, San Diego State University's president emeritus observed, "We had a cultural tension in that in the world of big box retail things are maintained at a high level. You wouldn't find a scrap of paper on the floor of a big box store." He recalled a situation where Price Philanthropies' "business" approach was a bit different from the approach of the university and its public education partners. He explained,

> [A Price Philanthropies senior staff member] had a set of eyes that could see everything. He would see things that an ordinary educator would glance over. There's a van parked and its windshield was cracked—must get it fixed. . . . There was a higher expectation and standard than we [in public education] were used to maintaining. It was not a problem or even a challenge but it had to be intentional.

Director Stewardship

Although Loyola Maryland, Seattle University, and the University of San Diego all had strong presidential backing for their initiatives, including support for fund development, during the development phase the directors of these initiatives provided significant leadership with external fund-raising. Each director faced the pressure and challenge of needing to secure external funding to grow their initiatives. During the development phase, the executive director of Seattle University's initiative began to devote almost 50% of his time to fund development. As the York Road Initiative developed, Loyola Maryland's director wrote a grant a week. As these examples demonstrate, many directors of traditional service-learning offices may experience significant shifts in focus as they develop place-based strategies.

In intensely pursuing external funding, campus directors of place-based initiatives formed more significant partnerships with their university's fund development divisions. Early in Seattle University's development phase the university's advancement division developed a position, senior director of development for community initiatives, to bolster efforts to acquire funding. Over the course of several years, this individual became an essential partner with the Center for Community Engagement, particularly the center's director. The senior director of development and the center director developed an effective strategy of inviting potential donors to participate in a walking tour of the Youth Initiative neighborhood to directly experience the university-community connections. This approach also helped surface the interests and passions of each prospective donor, enabling staff to follow up with tailored opportunities to give. The center director and several other center staff also played a significant role in supporting Seattle Housing Authority's successful pursuit of a $30 million federal Choice Neighborhood grant. As part of the grant, Seattle University receives funds to track data and evaluate the educational progress of neighborhood children.

Community and government relations partnerships framed Loyola Maryland's fund development strategies. As Loyola Maryland's director explained, "We have a small number of nonprofits here, so we have to coordinate [seeking grants]. If we don't, we end up competing against each other, and we don't utilize our energy as best as we can." With this perspective in mind, Loyola Maryland's director partnered with many nonprofits and city agencies to collectively acquire financial resources to implement its initiative. This approach reflects Loyola Maryland's focus on the development of its local commercial corridor, a significant difference from Seattle University and the University of San Diego's emphasis on education.

At the University of San Diego, deciding not to pursue a grant opened up new possibilities. Initially the director of the Mulvaney Center for Community, Awareness and Social Action planned to seek another major federal grant from the Department of Housing and Urban Development, but after thoroughly examining the institution's needs versus what the grant would provide, he decided to not reapply for funding. This decision led to more innovation within the office and lasting partnerships that have been critical to the university's place-based initiative.

Organizational Structures and Personnel: Building Infrastructure

Healthy organizations are often marked by their ability to be agile and responsive in the face of change, and universities are no different. During this time of rapid experimentation and change, campus units facilitating place-based initiatives often go through a period of assessing organizational structures and personnel. If resources and political will exist, staff roles and organizational structures begin to change. As the institutions that we examined suggest, institutional context matters greatly in how organizational change manifests itself. For many community engagement offices, the need for organizational redevelopment as an initiative develops is not a surprise; however, the slow pace of change and the emotional aspects arising from these changes are often underestimated.

Organizational Structures

The Pace of Change and the Positioning of Place-Based Leaders

Organizational change in place-based community engagement often depends on two key contextual factors: presidential leadership and the campus culture of change. For Drexel University and San Diego State University, creating a new organizational infrastructure occurred quickly and included one or more cabinet-level members responsible for the initiative but for contextually different reasons.

At Drexel University, the president's inaugural speech set the tone for university-community engagement and effectively set in motion his plan to establish a new position of senior vice provost for university and community partnerships who would be part of the presidential cabinet and direct the place-based initiative. At San Diego State University, President Weber, after deciding to partner with Price Philanthropies to improve City Heights, began to assemble a team of cabinet-level administrators including an associate provost and the College of Education dean to join him on the City Heights Initiative. President Emeritus Weber described his team, noting:

> I was not the brains of the operation. . . . Real educational expertise came from the dean of the college of education and financial expertise came from the associate provost. The associate provost controls 75% of the budget and was financial officer for the budget. The college of education dean understood education and schools. [He] could grasp what the question or problem was—sometimes you have a problem that you can't agree to what the solution is, but he could translate from K–12 jargon into higher education jargon.

The other three institutions in our study did not have a cabinet-level administrator leading their respective initiatives; each was led by an executive director/director-level administrator who reported to a cabinet member. In addition, at these institutions, the pace of organizational change was slower than at Drexel and San Diego State University. During the development phase at Seattle University, the director's title shifted to *executive director*. At Loyola Maryland, the York Road Initiative became a part of the Center for Community Service and Justice, and the York Road director became the leader of the entire unit. At the University of San Diego, the assistant director of the Mulvaney Center for Community, Awareness and Social Action was promoted to director when the prior director retired during the development phase.

Engagement of University Legal Counsel
During the development phase of their place-based initiatives, all five institutions that we studied had frequent conversations with their university legal counsel. This was especially true for institutions that started their initiatives in part due to safety issues. For example, during our joint interview with Drexel's executive director of the Dornsife Center (off-campus community center run by the university) and the executive director of the Lindy Center (on-campus student service-learning and community-based research center) we asked what other campus offices they worked closely with during the development phase. The executive directors looked at each other and laughed and then said, "Legal counsel." The Dornsife Center executive director explained further,

> We used to have weekly and then biweekly calls with legal counsel when we were developing programs. I had an event where legal counsel wanted community members to sign long consent forms and we had to work hard to educate them and make it more reasonable for community members to engage in an event and still have legal counsel satisfied that they had adequate risk management.

Staff from Loyola Maryland, Seattle University, San Diego State University, and the University of San Diego also had occasional meetings with legal counsel to review partnership agreements, develop background check protocols, or prepare for special events.

Collective Impact Approach
All of the institutions in our study used collective impact to develop their initiatives. Yet, in utilizing collective impact, the institutions played different types of roles, including (a) traditional anchor (Drexel), (b) convener (Seattle University and San Diego State University), and (c) government and community relations facilitator (Loyola Maryland and the University of San Diego).

Drexel, with President Fry utilizing community engagement to drive the entire institution's strategy, took a greater role as an anchor institution, although within the geography of its place-based initiative. During its development phase Drexel emerged as a national leader in using community engagement as a platform to pursue partnership work with schools as well as economic, housing, and workforce development.

In using collective impact, Seattle University has played a convener role in its local neighborhood and nationally. Through our focus group conversations, numerous community partners noted Seattle University's strength in connecting organizations with each other. Nationally, during its development phase, Seattle University began to convene other universities interested in place-based community engagement, including hosting several multiday institutes sponsored by the Annie E. Casey Foundation.

San Diego State University also has played a collective impact convener role, albeit in a somewhat different manner from Seattle University. During this phase, San Diego State University's Consensus Organizing Center worked to develop grassroots community leaders through education and training in the consensus organizing model, "a method of community organizing that focuses on finding and developing areas of mutual self-interest between community stakeholders, as opposed to traditional conflict-based organizing strategies" (Consensus Organizing Center, n.d.). As part of a collaboration with Price Philanthropies, the Consensus Organizing Center provided a space to bring together multiple community-centered opportunities, including programs and partnerships addressing safety and college access for foster youth.

Loyola Maryland and the University of San Diego engaged in government and community relations work through their collective impact approach. As noted earlier in this chapter, during its development phase Loyola Maryland pursued connections and collaborations with local and city government. This became the focal point of their collective impact approach. At the University of San Diego, the leadership of the place-based initiative used community and government relations tools to advocate for community organizations. More specifically, the University of San Diego explored how to leverage their resources to support existing community organizations above and beyond partnering on a program, in particular with the Linda Vista Planning Group (Linda Vista Planning Group, n.d.).

Building a Center for Partnerships
During the development phase, some place-based initiatives created a physical space for the community and university to come together for programming and events. In 2012, Drexel, with a major gift from Dana and David Dornsife (philanthropists who have generously supported higher education at a number of institutions), formed the Dornsife Center for Neighborhood Partnerships. Once a vacant building, this 29,400-square-foot space

functions as an "urban extension center" that allows Drexel's 15 colleges and schools to engage in service-learning and other community engagement programming within the community. An impressive space with an equally impressive array of programs, the Dornsife Center has multiple foci: adult education and workforce training, arts and culture, health and wellness, children and families, educational opportunities, and individual and family supports (Drexel University Dornsife Center for Neighborhood Partnerships, n.d.).

The Dornsife Center artfully unites the old and new—historical architecture with modern technological elements and the long-term residents of the community with the new students from the university. The Beachell Family Learning Center, which offers workforce support and development programs, provides a free-access "keyspot" computer lab for neighborhood residents. Dornsife's Community Lawyering Clinic, a partnership with the Drexel Law School, provides services such as direct representation and referrals in areas like criminal record expungement and employment discrimination. Youth and families from the community frequently use the community kitchen and the library iPad kiosk, a partnership with the Philadelphia public libraries, which allows community members to borrow iPads to read electronic books and periodicals.

Office and Building Name Changes
The name of an office or space is a significant identifier, especially for a place-based community engagement initiative. Names can imply the size, scope, vision, and values of an initiative. The institutions that we studied pursued two forms of name changes: office name changes and the naming of buildings. As noted in the previous section, Drexel University named their physical partnership center after the generous donation from the Dornsife family.

During their development phases, Seattle University and the University of San Diego changed office names to better reflect their place-based strategies. In recognizing that the broader moniker of community engagement more fully encapsulates the vision of the place-based approach, in 2015 Seattle University's Center for Service and Community Engagement became simply the Center for Community Engagement. The University of San Diego in 2002 changed the Office of Community Service-Learning to the *Center* for Community Service-Learning (our emphasis, not the center's) and then changed the name again in 2014 to the Mulvaney Center for Community, Awareness and Social Action (Jennewein, 2014), a name that reflects its broad approach to connecting campus and community.

Personnel

As the leaders and frontline individuals who represent the university in the community and on campus, the staff of a place-based community engagement initiative is an essential factor for success. During this phase, several major personnel issues that emerged included guiding and supporting existing staff and hiring and on-boarding new staff.

Existing Staff

Since most place-based initiatives are housed in existing community engagement offices the movement toward a placement-based approach created challenges in the universities we studied, particularly for existing staff. These individuals brought unique strengths to their initiative including institutional memory, campus and community relationships, and an understanding of institutional and community cultures. Yet the rapid change and shift in focus proved unsettling for some staff. Our research suggests that the changes arising from a new focus on place-based engagement can empower most staff, yet be off-putting for a few. During the development phase one of the most common personnel issues was how existing staff would pivot into new roles and responsibilities as part of the more expansive work of the initiative.

The challenge of guiding the change process for staff often fell under the purview of director-level administrators. At Seattle University, the executive director took an empathetic approach to staff development in the face of rapid and sometimes chaotic change, offering particular support to existing staff. Although patience was central to this process, navigating the tensions arising when staff members did not get promoted or disagreed with leadership decisions proved difficult. On several occasions staff morale suffered because of lack of role clarity and an inability to fully predict the direction of the organization. The executive director attempted to address these issues by providing additional professional development, team-building exercises, and a consultant to conduct an organizational analysis and make recommendations.

At two institutions, the director and senior leadership had to make tough decisions, including terminating and encouraging staff members to leave. As one executive leader shared, "There was one [senior administrator] who was not interested in doing this [community engagement work]. As a [senior leader] of the university, it was my responsibility to take care of that problem." In this case, a new senior administrator was hired, one with significant community engagement experience, so that the university could engage in partnership work with a strong leader. In another example, an individual who didn't have the skill set or interest in moving in a new direction was encouraged to leave, which the individual chose to do. When staff left, other individuals had the opportunity to join the team and bring their unique assets to the work.

Adding New Community Engagement Staff Members
During the development phase, most of the institutions we studied created an important new position of community engagement manager, an individual who is mostly off the university campus and in the community to create, manage, or repair partnerships. San Diego State University was the one exception, as it did not have a centralized service office that had reenvisioned itself for community engagement like the other institutions (see Table 5.2).

In addition, during the development phase, most of the institutions we studied also added additional off-site positions that operated under the auspices of the place-based initiative. Most of these positions were connected to school-based partnerships. For example, at San Diego State University, the College Avenue Compact student and nonstudent staff were employed through the university while they worked exclusively at various K–12 school sites. At Seattle University, a school success coordinator worked almost entirely at the local elementary school, and a parent engagement coordinator also focused almost solely on off-campus activities. Seattle University also employed a number of AmeriCorps members who served at various school sites.

The End of the Development Phase

The institutionalization of the initiative marks a key indicator of the end of the development phase. At the university, institutionalization means campus-wide awareness of the initiative, including the ability for faculty, staff, and

TABLE 5.2
Community Engagement Managers by Institution

University	Title
Drexel University	Executive director of the Dornsife Center for Neighborhood Partnerships
Loyola University Maryland	Assistant director for the York Road Initiative
Seattle University	Deputy director, Center for Community Engagement
San Diego State University	N/A
University of San Diego	Director of community-based youth programs

students to generally describe the initiative's purpose and activities. In the community, institutionalization implies a critical mass of community members engaged in the initiative's partnerships and the ability for a core group of community leaders to describe the initiative's vision and goals. The thorough development of major new partnerships or the attainment of substantial new funding are also signs of the initiative's institutionalization.

Each of the institutions that we studied reached an end to their development phases, although the indicators looked somewhat different. For example, Drexel's establishment of the Dornsife Center for Neighborhood Partnerships marked the end of its development phase, whereas Seattle University's development phase ended after the Seattle Housing Authority successfully attained the Choice Neighborhood grant with the university as a primary partner.

Lessons Learned From the Development Phase

The development phase of a place-based community engagement initiative produces a frenzy of activity, experimentation, and rapid change. Amid this intense period of time, institutions should continue to focus on thoughtful strategies. The lessons learned from the development phase include the following:

1. *Embrace experimentation and accept ambiguity.* The "spaghetti on the wall" nature of the development phase provides many opportunities for innovation and testing ideas. Although sometimes chaotic and unpredictable, these processes often lead to major new programs, partnerships, and funding opportunities. Leaders should celebrate this growth while accepting the lack of clarity inherent in this phase of the initiative.
2. *Accept that change will bring challenges.* The pace of change during the development phase will bring challenges. Organizational structures and staff will be stretched and leaders at all levels will need to stay focused on the overall goals of the initiative while also remaining attentive to the process of individual and organizational evolution.
3. *Relationships matter more than ever.* A centerpiece to the success of all five of the place-based initiatives we studied is the strong relationships between campus and community leaders at all levels. These relationships are particularly critical during the development phase as growth, uncertainty, and change test the resolve of all partners. Strong relationships with financial supporters that go beyond just the exchange of funding also contribute significantly to success.

Carefully considering these lessons and the many examples we have presented throughout this chapter sets the stage for universities and their communities to move their place-based community engagement initiative toward more stability and permanency. In the next chapter we examine the major factors that lead to a sustainable and long-term initiative.

Note

1. Drawing upon the work of critical race scholars in education (e.g., McCoy & Rodricks, 2015), we capitalize the term *People of Color* to acknowledge that this phrasing encompasses individuals from African American, Asian American, Latina/o, Native American, multiracial, and other self-identified individuals who do not exclusively identify as White.

6

THE SUSTAINING PHASE

In It for the Long Haul

As a place-based initiative attains relative stability and moves toward becoming a permanent part of the university and community, it enters the sustaining phase. Although innovation and creativity continue to contribute to deeper partnerships and programs, the sustaining phase brings maturation in strategy and implementation. The main goals of this phase are establishing longevity and pursuing continuous improvement. Among the institutions we studied, the key issues and topics that arose during the sustaining phase include gentrification, change management, sustainable programs and partnerships, and continuing to secure funding and resources. Unlike the other two phases, the sustaining phase has no endpoint (see Table 6.1).

Geographic Considerations: Managing Place in a Time of Gentrification

Place-based initiatives operate within much larger regional and national financial and economic systems. Over the past several decades, these economic forces have led to the influx of thousands of middle- and upper-income people into neighborhoods that have historically been inhabited by low-income residents (Maciag, 2015). Commonly referred to as *gentrification*, these trends may significantly impact place-based initiatives. In addition, the very success of place-based initiatives, especially with respect to housing and economic development, may contribute to gentrification.

All five of the institutions that we studied voiced significant concerns about gentrification. San Diego State University and Seattle University are experiencing gentrification in their neighborhoods, whereas Drexel,

TABLE 6.1

Place-Based Community Engagement: Sustaining Phase

	Start of Sustaining Phase	Initiative Director(s)	Cabinet-Level Initiative Representative
Drexel University	**2016** Applying for and receiving U.S. Department of Education Promise Neighborhood grant	Senior vice provost for university and community partnerships	President
Loyola University Maryland	**2016** Merger of the York Road Initiative and the Center for Community Service and Justice	Director, Center for Community Service and Justice	Vice president for administration
San Diego State University	**2011** Beginning of new president Elliot Hirshman's tenure	N/A	N/A
Seattle University	**2015** Proactively addressing gentrification; external funding reaches point of maturation	Executive director, Center for Community Engagement	Associate provost
University of San Diego	**2009** Beginning of external-facing director's work; start of new president James T. Harris III's tenure in 2015	Associate vice provost for community engagement	Provost

Loyola Maryland, and the University of San Diego have long-term concerns about the potential for gentrification within their communities.

Driven by fast economic growth, a thriving tech industry, and increasingly high housing costs, Seattle is in a state of rapid gentrification. *The Economist* recently labeled the region as "Silicon Valley North" (Silicon Valley North, 2017). In fact, Seattle has one of the highest rates of gentrification in the country (Maciag, 2015). Given the legacy of redlining and other racist housing policies, the city's historic African American community is particularly being negatively affected. As *Seattle Times* reporter Gene Balk notes, the difference between the first tech boom (Boeing in the 1970s) and the current one (Amazon, Microsoft, etc., in the 2000s) is African American home ownership. Home ownership among African Americans in King County, the county encompassing Seattle, has plummeted over the past 40 years (Balk, 2017). Today, African Americans make up only 20% of Seattle's Central District, the city's historic Black neighborhood, down from 70% in the 1970s (Beason, 2016). In Seattle, many low-income families and People of Color are being pushed out of the city to communities outside of the place-based initiative boundaries, where housing is more affordable but services and cultural institutions are limited.

Seattle University's place-based initiative includes a portion of the Central District as well as two other neighborhoods experiencing rapid transition, Yesler Terrace and the Chinatown-International District. Thus, the impacts of gentrification are a major concern and have led to adjustments to the Youth Initiative. Although continuing to focus primarily on the educational pathway of neighborhood children, the university has recently developed and expanded partnerships to address gentrification. For example, the Seattle University Innovation & Entrepreneurship Center, located at the Albers School of Business and Economics, has created a major new program to support neighborhood small businesses, particularly businesses owned by women, People of Color, and low-income residents. The university has also convened low-income housing providers and university faculty to strategize how best to deploy resources and advocate for publicly owned neighborhood properties to be used for low-income housing. Seattle University has also served as a core partner in the Yesler Community Collaborative, an effort to bring together "partners in the education, housing, environment, health care, business, arts, government and philanthropic sectors to support equitable and sustainable community development at Yesler Terrace and in surrounding neighborhoods" (Yesler Community Collaborative, n.d.). Finally, the deputy director of the Center for Community Engagement has participated in the Black Community Impact Alliance, an antigentrification effort focused on building the capacity and assets of Seattle's African American community.

Like Seattle University, San Diego State University's partnership with Price Philanthropies also encompasses a neighborhood experiencing gentrification. President Emeritus Weber spoke about the intentional effort to avoid contributing to gentrification. He shared:

> Price was smart about the type of housing and innovative programs to not gentrify the neighborhood. They helped to bring in businesses like grocery stores and improved the public infrastructure with public schools and a community center. They weren't bringing in high end retail or things like that.

Despite this intentionality, the new amenities in the neighborhood also made it more attractive to middle-income residents (Martinez-Cosio & Bussell, 2013).

Drexel, Loyola Maryland, and the University of San Diego are keenly aware of the risk of contributing to gentrification but also committed to improving the housing stock for local residents. For example, Loyola Maryland has partnered to move the local neighborhood from its "most distressed" federal status to "less distressed." One of Loyola Maryland's community partners shared that although gentrification can be an issue, "for this region it is still about getting rid of housing blight."

Within the York Road area condemned homes line a four-block area. In the middle of this area five homes are being rebuilt, a clear bright spot within a community where much more work is still needed. A community partner indicated his disappointment at the slower-than-anticipated pace of redevelopment:

> It has taken us longer to make these homes [that were being redeveloped] livable. We buy the homes for $10,000 from the city, but it can take more than $190,000 to repair them which is more than the home will be worth when it is completed.

Organizational Structures and Personnel: Change Management

During the sustaining phase, change remains a constant theme. Several of the institutions we studied experienced presidential transitions during their sustaining phases, and all of the institutions grappled with staff transitions and maintaining an appropriate organizational infrastructure.

Senior University Leadership

During the sustaining phase, San Diego State University and the University of San Diego both experienced a change in presidential leadership. For San

Diego State University, the presidential transition meant less innovation and fewer new programs but strong continued partnerships in the City Heights neighborhood. Since 2011, more than six years after President Emeritus Weber's retirement, many of the partnerships with Price Philanthropies and the City Heights area, especially with the San Diego Unified School District, continue to thrive.

As described in previous chapters, in 2015, the University of San Diego's appointment of James T. Harris III as president has amplified their place-based efforts. President Harris is using community engagement as a central element of his institution's strategic plan. Each area of the strategic plan touches upon community engagement. For example, the plan sets a goal to "emerge as the leading, faith-based anchor university in the United States" (University of San Diego, n.d.). Three of the plan's pathways to attain this goal connect to place-based community engagement: (a) becoming an anchor institution, (b) engaged scholarship, and (c) practice break at change-making (University of San Diego, n.d.). In addition, under President Harris's leadership the University of San Diego's place-based initiative has become more formalized within university structures, including a reorganization of the university's community engagement office that oversees the place-based initiative.

Although not experiencing presidential transitions, Loyola Maryland and Seattle University's place-based initiatives, both led by director-level administrators, have had changes in whom they report to within the university. At Seattle University, during the sustaining phase the executive director has reported to two different associate provosts and now reports to the interim provost. The Loyola Maryland director has also had shifts in supervision. Yet, in both cases, these changes have not led to major setbacks. For example, a cabinet-level administrator whom the Loyola Maryland's director reports to shared, "[The initiative] is an important element of who we are and what we do, and will continue to be in the next 5 to 10 years."

The solid and consistent success of Loyola Maryland and Seattle University's initiatives clearly play a role in managing these administrative reporting changes. In addition, each director's ability to form strong working relationships with supervisors has likely mitigated any negative impact of these structural changes.

Initiative Staff

For the institutions we studied, the staff changes that occurred in the development phase led to greater organizational maturity in the sustaining phase. Yet, although more stable, almost all of the place-based efforts experienced continued challenges in growing and developing staff amid the evolution of their initiatives.

The institutions within our study attained several noteworthy staffing and organizational successes during the sustaining phase. For example, one institution created a position of deputy director to guide the external strategy of its initiative, which helped to clarify decision-making processes. This person can fill in for the director and, from a succession planning standpoint, is ready to step in if and when the director leaves the initiative.

Most of the institutions in our study also expanded their efforts to create externally facing and, in several cases, off-site staff positions. The thoughtful integration of these staff into the initiative team significantly enhanced the potential for success. Reflecting on the benefits of the external/off-site staff member, the leader of one initiative observed, "I can see how we have stronger relationships with our school partners—there is less miscommunication now that [the off-site staff member] has been with us for a while."

During the sustaining phase, two of the institutions experienced their main external/off-site staff members leaving the institution. Although these departures were unrelated to performance, the departures did impact institutional initiatives. One director shared,

> [The staff member] has such strong relationships with the community.
> I am scared when [the staff member] leaves how it will impact our partnerships . . . and even if I replace [the staff member] it will take a while for our partners to warm up.

In addition, for the institutions in our study, hiring and on-boarding a new externally facing staff member proved somewhat challenging, as most of the time these individuals came from outside of higher education (e.g., nonprofit and other community contexts) and not from within the university. This required different types of on-boarding, training, development, and socialization to the university in order to integrate and retain such staff members.

Programs and Engagement: Moving Toward Sustainability

The sustaining phase often brings greater stability and deeper quality for campus and community partnerships, governance structures, and fund development efforts. The incorporation of the initiative into the university strategic plan and the development of advisory boards provide deeper links to the overall institution. The creation of signature programs that symbolize the initiative become more and more prevalent. Many initiatives develop new academic and cocurricular programs that further strengthen ties between the university and the community.

Strategic Plans and Advisory Boards

A university's strategic plan highlights the priorities of the institution for the foreseeable future and therefore the inclusion of the place-based initiative in the plan demonstrates how the effort fits into the institution's overall direction. In fact, President Linnane of Loyola Maryland observed that to attain success, the "initiative must advance the strategic plan." As noted earlier, Drexel and the University of San Diego chose to build their overall strategic plan around their place-based focus. Seattle University and Loyola Maryland's plans highlighted their place-based initiative among a set of several major goals and objectives.

In addition to strategic plans, well-designed advisory boards also provide an important means to further embed the place-based initiative within the fabric of the institution. Seattle University has utilized several boards to guide its place-based initiative, including a board consisting of 16 campus and community leaders that advises staff on strategy and partnerships. Seattle University also has a task force assisting with the initiative's fund development efforts. Finally, building upon the informal "kitchen cabinet" that offered him guidance during the exploratory and development phases, during the sustaining phase the executive director has met every other month with an executive advisory board of 5 people that offers insights on trends and emerging issues related to the Youth Initiative. Several university trustees or former trustees serve on these various boards which enables the initiative to further connect with the university's governance structure.

Signature Programs

Each of the institutions in our study have developed signature programs as part of their initiatives. In previous chapters we have highlighted some of these programs, including a farmer's market (the University of San Diego and Loyola Maryland) and Community Engagement Center (Drexel University's Dornsife Center). Several institutions pursued signature programs that create what the president emeritus of San Diego State University calls a "virtuous cycle"—long-term programs that serve community members who then enroll at the university and give back to their own communities, in many instances becoming leaders of the community (see Figure 6.1).

Although taking many years to develop, Seattle University and San Diego State both pursued programs and partnerships that created a virtuous cycle. Seattle University has developed a cradle-to-career pathway for

Figure 6.1. Place-based community engagement virtuous cycle.

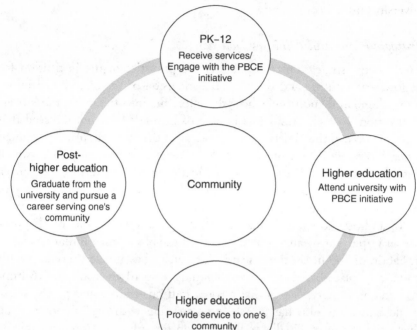

neighborhood youth, including after-school programs, summer activities, and mentoring projects. As it entered the sustaining phase, Seattle University built upon its successful partnership at Bailey Gatzert Elementary School to expand programming and partnerships at Washington Middle School. This includes the creation of a comprehensive mentoring program that mobilizes university students to serve as academic mentors for Bailey Gatzert Elementary School students who matriculate to Washington Middle School. The university has also expanded support for high school students, including supporting a Summer Youth Media program that trains local high school students to document the redevelopment of a large public housing community in the Youth Initiative neighborhood.

With these programs and partnerships in place, Seattle University is also developing a scholarship program that currently enables two to three neighborhood youths per year to attend the university with no or very limited expenses. In addition to these scholarship recipients, several more neighborhood students have also enrolled at the university and, as college students, have become involved in the Youth Initiative. One local student even began volunteering during the summer before she started her freshman year at the university, and several students have served in neighborhood schools and organizations during their entire college experience. One of these students has graduated and is now working for a neighborhood organization.

San Diego State University's College Avenue Compact, a collaboration among the university, the San Diego Unified School District, and Price Philanthropies, represents an example of a complete virtuous cycle. Over many years the College Avenue Compact has created a comprehensive college access program engaging City Heights students and families in high-quality college preparatory opportunities. At present, students attending Hoover High School, the neighborhood high school, are eligible to receive guaranteed admission and a full tuition scholarship to San Diego State University if they fulfill the requirements of the program (Making College Possible, n.d.):

- Complete the 15-unit "a–g" college preparatory course requirements
- Maintain a 3.0 GPA in "a–g" college preparatory courses
- Take the SAT or ACT
- Satisfy placement tests (the San Diego State University Entry Level Mathematics Test and San Diego State University English Placement Test)
- Pass the California High School Exit Exam

The program has matured quite a bit since its initial implementation. Today, students receive mentorship from "hometown college students," San Diego State University students who participated in the program or are from City Heights. The students also receive college counseling to keep them on track academically. Recently, the College Avenue Compact has expanded to the middle schools that feed into Hoover High School, building upon research that college preparation needs to start early (Making College Possible, n.d.). Parent engagement has also become a key component of the program. Parents and family members have the opportunity to participate in college awareness and financial aid workshops, advising sessions, college campus tours, a parent ambassadors program, and a college home visit program (Making College Possible, n.d.). As the executive director of College Avenue Compact shared, there's a lot of innovation by including parents in the college preparatory experience:

> We conduct home visits in pairs, we have parents watch a video and review their child's transcript. They have an opportunity to ask questions. We discuss their college dreams and how they might support their children. This is especially important because most of our students are the first in their families to go to college.

Students can also participate in additional enrichment activities, summer programs, and field trips to the university. Some of the students who participated in the program in high school have now graduated from San Diego State University and work with the College Avenue Compact and in other educational programs.

San Diego State University's social work partnership contributes to this virtuous cycle that links with the work of the College Avenue Compact. Through this partnership, high school students from City Heights can take a course in social work to better understand the systemic forces impacting their community and the resources to support its well-being. Once students use their College Avenue Compact scholarship to begin at San Diego State University, they can participate in social work internships in City Heights. Upon graduation, many students choose to work as social workers in the community and some even return to San Diego State University to get a graduate degree in social work. The director noted that one community leader worked for San Diego State University after she received her bachelor's and master's degrees from the university and now works with Price Philanthropies to continue supporting the virtuous cycle that connects City Heights and San Diego State University.

Course Institutionalization

Developing university courses and curricula that focus on neighborhood issues is an essential strategy to sustain place-based community engagement initiatives. This curricular connection can engage hundreds of students over many years in understanding community issues. There is also potential to democratize ownership of the initiative among university faculty, making it less dependent on the initiative's staff and director. Although taking many months and often involving an arduous internal review process, all of the institutions we studied created courses and curricula related to their initiatives. The types and forms of these curricula varied widely and involved undergraduate, graduate, and professional students as well as community leaders and residents.

Elective Courses
Seattle University partners with the Interdisciplinary Liberal Studies Program in the College of Arts and Sciences to offer several elective courses. One of these courses focuses on teaching in a multicultural context and is cotaught by a local school administrator and university staff person on site at a local elementary school. Through the course students serve and learn in the school and engage teachers, administrators, and parents through guest lectures and discussion. Another course explores the ethics and

politics of university engagement in communities and requires students to serve at Youth Initiative–affiliated partners. Although staff members from the Center for Community Engagement have taught these courses, at the present time teaching is not a part of their primary job description—it is optional.

The University of San Diego's School of Leadership and Education Sciences offers a leadership course focusing on school partnerships in the Linda Vista neighborhood. Reflecting on the development of the course one of the instructors shared, "We were the first to ask to partner with a school to teach this type of course. And other colleges started to offer this type of course after us." The course has gone through multiple iterations. Initially, it focused on reflection sections and helping the students process their service-learning experiences. However, student learning was, in the assessment of one of the instructors, "two inches deep and not as transformative as expected." In the sustaining phase, the course curriculum has solidified and now focuses on the students' development and self-awareness, including the ability to constructively engage issues of racism, systemic privilege, and the consequences of inaction. Attending to students' multicultural and relational competence, the course aims to help students grow and transform through their service-learning experiences.

First-Year/University 101 Courses
Drexel currently offers multiple sections of a first-year course on civic engagement. In offering these first-year experiences, Drexel strives to introduce students to the community where they will have additional curricular and cocurricular opportunities to engage throughout their college careers. Yet it is important to note that although course development is a key method of institutionalizing an initiative, it is a slow process. The executive director of the Lindy Center explained:

> President John Fry came to Drexel and boldly announced that he wanted Drexel to be civically engaged along several dimensions including academic integration, student and employee volunteerism, and institutional investment. We took the opportunity to draft a syllabus for a one-credit course that would focus singularly on civic engagement, effectively breaking it out from the UNIV 101 course and creating CIVC 101. After about a year of back and forth with faculty senate, and with the support of a college that signed on to be an early adopter (College of Arts & Sciences), we had the course formally approved. It took another two years to ramp the course up to serve all students across the university. . . . Today, all traditional undergraduate students have CIVC 101 as a required course within their first-year curriculum.

Civic Engagement Certificate

In addition to its first-year courses, Drexel also offers a civic engagement certificate. Students who earn the civic engagement certificate complete 18 units of coursework, including the following:

CIVC 100: Foundations of Civic Engagement

CIVC 201: Active Citizenship

CIVC 202: University-Community Partnerships

CIVC 203: Civic Engagement Leadership

CIVC 490: Civic Engagement Capstone Project

The civic engagement certificate offers students a chance to deeply engage in the community and culminates in a capstone project.

Clinical Experiences/Internships

Loyola Maryland and San Diego State University offer clinical experiences for undergraduate and graduate students at off-site community-based centers. As noted earlier, San Diego State University's School of Social Work provides undergraduate students with clinical opportunities to develop workshops and other programs at Hoover High School in the City Heights neighborhood. In addition, San Diego State University places interns at the City Heights Center for Community Counseling and Engagement, a one-stop social service center for City Heights residents that offers free and reduced-rate counseling. Through the College of Education, San Diego State University also offers school counseling internships at City Heights elementary, middle, and high schools.

Opportunities for Community Members to Take Courses

Curricular innovations related to place-based initiatives are not solely designed for university students. Side-by-Side courses at Drexel and Open University courses at the University of San Diego provide community members with an opportunity to take courses at the university alongside the university students who are involved in community engagement.

Drawing upon the example of Temple University's highly acclaimed Inside-Out International Prison Exchange program, Drexel has developed a series of courses that offer community members a chance to take a course with Drexel students to cocreate solutions to social problems (Drexel University Lindy Center for Civic Engagement, n.d.). Taught by Drexel faculty, the Side-by-Side courses have partnered with community organizations focusing on a variety of issues, including urban farming, senior living, and minority-owned businesses. Side-by-Side courses have also been offered out of Drexel's

Dornsife Center for Community Partnerships. Neighborhood residents do not pay tuition to take the courses, and Drexel provides all course materials to residents at no cost.

At the University of San Diego, a faculty member in the School of Leadership and Education Sciences who believed that community members should have access to higher education and taking courses with university students created the Open University Initiative. The project, in close collaboration with the Bayside Community Center, invited participants as "community experts" to audit courses of their choice. As of the fall semester of 2016, 6 participants, 9 faculty members from across campus, and close to 130 University of San Diego students were impacted by the initiative. The faculty member shared,

> Open University really values the community members and my research shows that their rich life experiences contributed significantly to the development of new perspectives of the university students enrolled in the courses. It is definitely a two-way mutually beneficial learning endeavor.

Local Immersions

Recognizing that direct experiences often lead to intellectual exploration and thoughtful action, during its sustaining phase, Seattle University has offered a series of 1- to 3-day-long community immersions for faculty, staff, and community members to learn experientially about issues related to the Youth Initiative. In groups of 10 to 15 people, immersion participants learn about topics such as affordable housing, early learning, or health care through dialogue with community members; neighborhood walks; visits to local organizations; and direct experiences with nonprofit, cultural, and religious institutions. Not designed to offer a "service," the immersions provide participants with intensive learning opportunities that often lead to additional connections to university courses, research projects, and major university-wide initiatives. A significant byproduct of the immersions is the creation of new interdisciplinary and interoffice relationships that can foster additional innovative community engagement efforts.

Maturation of Resources and Funding

The longevity of a place-based community engagement initiative depends on having adequate resources and funding. In the sustaining phase, fund development remains an imperative. Yet, with more of a proven track record of success and the maturation of relationships with current and prospective funders, the fund development process becomes less haphazard, more long term, and much more nuanced.

Strategic Plan and Transformative Donors

The presence of the place-based initiative in the university's strategic plan often leads to the inclusion of the initiative in the university's fund development campaign. All of the institutions that we studied except for San Diego State University included their initiatives in their universities' campaigns. For example, Seattle University's current $300 million institution-wide campaign includes a $30 million subgoal for community engagement. This goal includes funds for an endowment of the Center for Community Engagement (where the initiative is housed), scholarships for neighborhood youth to attend the university, and support for other campus units. At the time of writing this book, the university has received several major gifts toward this ambitious goal.

Several institutions that we studied received transformational gifts that significantly strengthened their place-based initiatives. The University of San Diego received a major gift from the Mulvaney family, which led to renaming the university's community engagement center. In addition, the university amplified the Mulvaney gift through a matching challenge that raised another $450,000 for the center from additional donors (Jennewein, 2014). As noted in the previous chapter, Drexel received a $10 million gift from the Dornsife family to develop the Dornsife Center for Community Partnerships, which fueled Drexel's movement to focusing more on community impact. The success of this endeavor led the Dornsifes to make an additional gift of $45 million to the Drexel School of Public Health, which is now also named after the Dornsife family (DrexelNOW, n.d.). Drexel's partnership with the Dornsife family illustrates how a place-based initiative can be a catalyst for a donor to get to know the institution, which can lead to even larger gifts in the future.

External Funding Amplification

During the sustaining phase, institutions that have successfully implemented a place-based initiative can begin to have success in attaining support from national foundations and the federal government. For example, after learning about the Seattle University Youth Initiative through a major competitive grant process, the Annie E. Casey Foundation engaged Seattle University in funding the development of a network of colleges and universities pursuing place-based initiatives.

In addition, because of its stellar track record of community engagement in West Philadelphia and because of its ambitious future plans with community partners, in 2016 the federal Department of Education awarded Drexel and its partners a 5-year, $30 million Promise Neighborhood grant. This is a tremendous honor for Drexel as only a handful of institutions in the country have received this highly competitive grant (Seal, 2016).

San Diego State University: One Lead Funder

The fund development strategy for San Diego State University was different from other institutions that we studied. Throughout all phases of its initiative, San Diego State University has partnered primarily with one philanthropic organization, Price Philanthropies. Recognizing that the partnership with Price would not last forever, during the sustaining phase San Diego State University began to explore other ways to fund its City Heights partnerships or begin institutionalizing practices without external funding. For example, the School of Social Work solidified its City Heights practicum and internship opportunities with the leveling off of initial funding from Price Philanthropies. For its part, Price Philanthropies has continued to invest in San Diego State University's efforts while also beginning to work with other institutions of higher education and other partners to support the full spectrum of efforts to improve the City Heights community.

Hallmarks of Long-Term Sustainability

The sustaining phase of place-based community engagement does not have an endpoint as programs, partnerships, and funding relationships continue to evolve and change. Yet, drawing upon the institutional examples from this chapter, several specific characteristics provide a sense of an initiative's ability to continue to thrive over the long term. These hallmarks of a place-based initiative's long-term sustainability include the following:

1. *Having significant community benefits and results.* What makes place-based community engagement somewhat different from traditional service-learning and other ubiquitous university-led community engagement efforts is the equal emphasis on campus and community impact. Place-based initiatives will flourish if they consistently attain positive community results. This is not to say campus impact is not important; it is essential. But if the community does not experience benefits from the place-based approach, the initiative will likely not continue. Part of pursuing positive results means carefully monitoring for progress in areas such as high-quality affordable housing, educational attainment, economic opportunities, or health.

2. *Being able to support and partner with changing neighborhoods.* By focusing on specific geographic areas, universities pursuing place-based initiatives are significantly impacted by changes in their communities. Gentrification can challenge the community and the campus. How institutions navigate the ethics and politics of gentrification will determine the viability and success of the initiative and can also have profound positive or negative impacts on neighborhoods.

3. *Becoming part of the university strategic plan.* Successfully embedding the initiative in the university strategic plan leads to focused attention from university leadership, trustees, and funders. Creating advisory boards and other structures to engage all levels of the campus and community in guiding the initiative democratizes ownership of the initiative, making it less vulnerable to changes in leadership or funding.

4. *Making creative curricular connections.* Thoughtfully linking the initiative to academic programs and courses significantly enhances student and faculty involvement, strengthens the university learning environment, and, because of the slow nature of curriculum change, provides semi-permanent partnerships between campus and community. Developing impactful signature partnerships or programs provides the initiative with consistent visibility and concrete examples of the initiative at work. In addition, the initiative itself can become a vehicle for curricular innovation that moves well beyond traditional service-learning to community members taking courses with students and students enrolling in certificate and academic degree programs that are based in the community.

5. *Attaining a "virtuous cycle."* By supporting local youth during their K–12 education, providing scholarships to attend the university, and mobilizing them to engage in their neighborhood as undergraduates, place-based initiatives can foster additional community leaders who can have transformative effects on the neighborhood and the university. A long-term indicator of an initiative's success might be the presence of university graduates who grew up in the local neighborhood working with the initiative or leading local organizations.

6. *Managing transitions and investing in initiative leadership.* Transitions in university presidents and upper-level administration, changes in the staffing of place-based initiatives, and shifts in the leadership of community organizations are almost a given. Remembering that trusting and strong relationships are the heart of place-based initiatives will help manage these major shifts. In addition, fostering pathways for staff to advance

and grow professionally will strengthen an initiative's long-term prospects and create a natural plan for leadership succession.

7. *Pursuing reciprocal and long-term funding partnerships.* Much like faculty, students, and community partners, funding partners can be invited to deepen and enhance their engagement in the place-based initiative. Through this process funders will better understand the initiative's opportunities and challenges and become more strategic in their giving. For some funders, the opportunity to learn and grow through the initiative can lead to paradigm shifts and significant individual and organizational transformation.

8. *Engaging in learning networks.* No institution, initiative, or community has all the answers to the challenges of creating positive campus and community change. Participating in learning networks, whether among community organizations or multiple universities, creates opportunities for continued learning and a reminder that place-based efforts are linked to much larger social movements. For some institutions, leading networks of other universities provides a mechanism not only for influencing their campus or local community but also the nation.

These eight hallmarks of long-term sustainability can serve as guideposts for universities and their communities. By periodically taking stock of their initiative and returning to these fundamentals, leaders can successfully guide their place-based community engagement efforts to attain transformational results. Yet, as noted throughout this book, initiatives driven solely by the college or university will struggle and face many challenges. Community leaders provide essential guidance and leadership. The next chapter presents lessons and examples of place-based community engagement from the perspective of community partners.

PART THREE

KEY CONSIDERATIONS
FOR PRACTICE

7

A VIEW FROM THE COMMUNITY

Community Partners' Perspectives

Community partners are an integral component of place-based community engagement, especially in moving toward equally emphasizing campus and community impact. During our site visits to the five communities and institutions included in our study we met with approximately 85 community partners from many sectors, including education, low-income housing, community development, and city government. Through these conversations we began to recognize the wide spectrum of types of partnerships and organizations that make place-based community engagement successful. A common theme among all of the varied partners was a strong willingness to engage with the place-based initiative in order to pursue deep and long-lasting community change.

In this chapter, we highlight partners that exemplify the dozens of community partners engaging with the five institutions that we studied. We subsequently draw upon the viewpoints of some of these community partners to share promising practices for reciprocal partnerships in place-based community engagement. These practices include building trust, communicating effectively, working through problems that emerge, addressing the diversity of the community, and creating the virtuous cycle of engagement.

Although we met with community members who were engaged with the Dornsife Center, we were unable to visit external community partners during our visit to Drexel University. Thus, we share our findings from Loyola University Maryland, San Diego State University, Seattle University, and the University of San Diego, as well as from our visit to Drexel's Dornsife Center.

Types of Community Partners

A wide range of community partners participate in place-based community engagement with their local institutions of higher education. Drawing upon the five institutions and communities that we visited, in the following section we share examples of partners within specific categories, including national organizations, local nonprofits, religious and faith-based institutions, schools, government partners, elected officials, and philanthropists.

National Organizations

- *Habitat for Humanity.* Loyola Maryland has partnered with the Chesapeake branch of this national organization that works toward neighborhood revitalization through partnerships with homebuyers, volunteers, donors, businesses, and community organizations. Habitat for Humanity is well known for its model of "sweat equity," in which future homebuyers contribute labor in the construction of their homes.
- *Local Initiatives Support Corporation (LISC).* The Philadelphia branch of the LISC has played a lead role in organizing community input and advising Drexel's work in the Mantua and Powelton Village neighborhoods.

Local Nonprofit Organizations

- *Bayside Community Center.* On issues from housing to education to food security, Bayside has served as a key partner in the University of San Diego's place-based engagement efforts in Linda Vista.
- *Strong City Baltimore.* A nonprofit organization in Baltimore that has served as a key partner with Loyola Maryland, especially with its housing and education initiatives in north Baltimore.

Religious and Faith-Based Organizations

- *Catholic Churches and Schools.* Loyola Maryland has various partnerships with local Catholic churches and schools, including Cristo Rey Jesuit High School, St. Ignatius Loyola Academy, St. Paul Bridges Program, and St. Vincent de Paul's Beans and Bread Outreach Center.
- *Catholic Community Services Village Spirit Center.* Seattle University has partnered with the Village Spirit Center to provide culturally and racially specific programming in the Central District and combat the negative effects of gentrification.

K–12 Schools

- *Bailey Gatzert Elementary School, Seattle Public Schools.* Every year since 2010, Seattle University undergraduates have supported classroom learning and facilitated an extended learning program at Bailey Gatzert Elementary School.
- *Montgomery Middle School, San Diego Unified School District.* The University of San Diego provides leadership of the counseling program at Montgomery Middle School by placing paid interns and faculty on site to support teachers and students.
- *Rosa Parks Elementary School, San Diego Unified School District.* For more than 15 years, graduate students from San Diego State University's College of Education and School of Social Work have served as interns in classrooms and clinical settings at Rosa Parks Elementary School.

Federal/State/City Partners

- *United States Department of Education and the City of Philadelphia.* Drexel, the Philadelphia School District, and the city of Philadelphia are partnering with the Department of Education through a $6 million Promise Neighborhood grant.
- *United States Department of Housing and Urban Development and Seattle Housing Authority.* Seattle University is the lead education partner in Seattle Housing Authority's $30 million Choice Neighborhood grant from the Department of Housing and Urban Development.

Elected Officials

- *City Council Member.* Loyola Maryland has a strong partnership with City Council member Bill Henry, District 4 in Baltimore, Maryland.

Philanthropy

- *Price Philanthropies.* Throughout San Diego State University's 20-year partnership with the City Heights neighborhood, Price Philanthropies has provided financial support and strategic leadership.
- *William Penn Foundation.* The William Penn Foundation provided $2.5 million to support Drexel's Promise Zone partnership.

Effective Practices

The community partners involved in the place-based initiatives that we studied named a number of promising practices that contributed to successful partnerships. These practices include building trust, communicating effectively, working through problems that emerge, addressing community diversity, and creating the virtuous cycle of engagement.

Building Trust

Many of the community partners we met with observed that trusting relationships with key university staff members provided the foundation for an effective and positive campus-community partnership. For example, a partner from Strong City Baltimore shared an example of trust that she had with Loyola Maryland's York Road Initiative director:

> Having a strong relationship with [the initiative director] is important. Trust is a big part of that. I know that when [the initiative director] comes to us with a proposal that she's here because it is in our best interest and she thinks it will add value to our organization and the community . . . or when I give her feedback that something isn't working the [initiative director] trusts that I'm coming from a good place.

Although trust is vital, many of the community partners we met with noted that it had to be earned through many years of collaboration. For example, a community partner from Bayside Community Center shared their experience with the University of San Diego:

> I've known [the director and the external relations manager] for a number of years. They are both stellar, people with a lot of integrity . . . and they have built up this kinship with us over many years, including other [senior staff] before me. . . . They have earned our trust.

Maintaining Clear and Continuous Communication

Community partners also highlighted the need for clear and continuous communication in order to have an effective and long-lasting partnership. One of Loyola Maryland's community partners from Govans Elementary School in Baltimore talked about this:

> Keeping each other in the loop is hard but important work. . . . Sometimes we do this over e-mail. I also see [Loyola Maryland staff members] at the school or community events or meetings. . . . For me, it's not how the information gets exchanged; it's that it does.

For another Loyola Maryland community member who has worked with the university for many years, listening and having the opportunity for input was also very important to the partnership.

The year of listening, the "Year of the City" was what the university called it. I thought it was done well; [the university administrator] brought forth concerns in a positive way, he understood the real need to partner with communities and was clear about interest—good at communicating Jesuit values to the community . . . and when it came time to hire someone, I said to hire someone who will be a strong advocate [and has experience with York Road], and he did.

During a focus group, several of Seattle University's community partners agreed that the university was a strong communicator. A school partner shared:

Communication goes pretty well—it's one that goes back and forth. What I've appreciated is when it's become difficult; we've regrouped and talked about how it could've gone better (should we meet every week, should we meet once a month, should we meet once a trimester). So, we've kind of finessed that. I appreciate that kind of resilience and making that better.

Members of the Seattle University Youth Initiative Advisory Board also highlighted the significance of Seattle University's communication strategy. One board member observed,

Early on, their website was not as strong. . . . Today, the website more clearly communicates the work to a generalist audience. There are e-mails. The glossy pictures in the office and in their fund-raising documents. The annual reports. Being highlighted in the [university] magazine. . . . They spend a good amount of time on sharing their story and work. Their ability to have solid partnerships and get external funding attests to their success.

Addressing Problems

Community partners across all institutions in our study shared that one very effective practice was the ability of their respective university partner to quickly and effectively address problems that arose in the partnership. These partners also noted that frequent check-ins and data sharing helped to address issues quickly or avoid them entirely. A Seattle University community partner with the College Success Foundation noted her experience:

There is one thing that Seattle University does uniquely well. When there is an issue that needs to be addressed immediately, they are responsive. We had a student issue and I got an e-mail and then [a] phone call within a couple of hours, and we were able to resolve this issue to the satisfaction of all parties.

A Seattle University community partner from the Seattle Housing Authority also shared:

> There is a clear understanding of roles . . . what the university does . . . what we [Seattle Housing Authority] do . . . and when we get together, there's a humility about the work that's so helpful when we run into an issue. . . . It's more about understanding and finding a solution.

Community partners also shed light on the effectiveness of quick feedback loops in addressing and mitigating problems. A community partner from Rosa Parks Elementary shared an experience with San Diego State University and Price Philanthropies. She observed how they are in communication about major data points—at the beginning of the year, at midyear, and at the end of the year. This school administrator kept a prominent visual representation in her office to remind her each day of where the school was with its outcomes, areas of focus, and so on. In particular, she displayed a colorful matrix of each classroom, each teacher, and every major student grouping in her office to use as part of her data-based decision-making; frequent communication about data was an important practice to share progress and challenges internally with her elementary school campus and externally with partners.

A school partner of Loyola Maryland observed how they gave feedback on a consistent basis:

> We have what I believe are quarterly meetings, where we sit down, share what is and what is not working, usually when the school year slows down some more, like after the [winter] holidays and spring break. It has been good to take this time to do this reflection work with each other to keep us accountable.

Navigating Diversity and Racially Mismatched Contexts

All of the institutions in our study are universities with predominantly White student populations. In addition, in all but one case (the University of San Diego) the majority of the staff of the place-based initiative are also White. Yet each of the place-based initiatives in our study partners with a community population that consists largely of People of Color. Community partners brought up this racially mismatched context, wherein the university staff and students are mostly White while their community members are People of Color. The partners noted the importance of carefully navigating the cross-cultural and diversity issues arising from this context.

A Seattle University partner from a community health organization discussed how training could be improved for students working in her community:

> Seattle University students are young compared to the adults we serve. And many of the White students have not had exposure to older African Americans. We've had a couple of situations where there were some assumptions made. . . . If they had more training with diversity before coming to us, it would be helpful.

A long-standing Loyola Maryland community partner talked about the importance of the campus engaging in the community but not from a "White savior" standpoint. She shared, "So much visioning that has been done with the community [by the director of the place-based initiative]. . . . Everything is done with community building in mind (not White savior); and there is a celebratory community." For this community partner, building upon community assets and centralizing celebration assisted with the navigation of some of the racial and cultural incongruity.

For the University of San Diego, even though many of their students and the majority of their place-based initiative staff are People of Color, navigating diversity concerns still arose as an issue. For example, one community partner discussed a case in which a University of San Diego faculty member drew upon a deficit perspective to describe the community to a student. In reflecting on the faculty member's comment, the partner observed, "What I want students to know is that it's not about just understanding social inequality; we want to empower people to deal with systemic issues of poverty . . . to challenge social justice energy to empower people to sustain themselves." This example highlights that to address racial and cultural issues, just training university students will not suffice. Universities must provide faculty with professional development opportunities that directly engage issues of race and culture and focus upon an asset-based approach to community partnerships.

The Virtuous Cycle

Community members also highlighted the relevance of the virtuous cycle that we described in chapter 6. However, community members had a slightly different angle on the phenomenon. Many community partners and university initiative staff members were alumni of the university prior to their professional positions. In fact, the directors of two initiatives (Loyola Maryland and the University of San Diego) were well-known undergraduate student leaders at their institutions prior to directing initiatives. For campus and community partners, this was an immense source of pride and community continuity. A faculty director at the University of San Diego shared her experience with the initiative director:

> I remember when [the director of the place-based initiative] was an undergraduate student in my classes and also so involved in leadership positions on campus. For him to be named the director was bringing his education full circle from student to professional . . . and to be engaged with the community the entire time.

A senior university administrator from Loyola Maryland noted, "To have a former student body president who we trained and then went to work in the community upon graduation to come back to lead this [initiative] is such a gift and testament to our education here at Loyola."

Community partners also lauded the "homegrown" status of these directors. A Loyola Maryland community partner shared that the director "was a leader back then [as an undergraduate student] and continues to lead now on a larger scale. . . . The work is in good hands." A University of San Diego community partner who is also an alumna and worked with the director of the initiative as a graduate student elaborated on this. "To have the [initiative director] also be an alumnus and former student leader, it makes me proud. I think it also reflects the continuing work he is doing to fulfill the mission and lead by example."

In addition to the leaders of the Loyola Maryland and University of San Diego initiatives, many additional staff of the place-based initiatives are also alumni. For example, four of the AmeriCorps members working with the Seattle University Youth Initiative are graduates of the university; two of these individuals are completing their second terms as AmeriCorps members at Bailey Gatzert Elementary School, after serving at the school during all four years of their undergraduate studies. Loyola Maryland also has had a number of recent graduates serve the York Road Initiative as AmeriCorps members, including one individual who later transitioned to become a full-time staff member with the initiative.

Community partners who attended one of the institutions in our study were quick to share their alumni status and pride in their alma maters. The continued contribution of these former students to the communities in which they were engaged as students illustrates the virtuous cycle of alumni (see chapter 6 for more details on the virtuous cycle). At the University of San Diego, the majority of community partners we met during our site visits were alumni. At Loyola Maryland, several alumni are now full-time professionals in local community organizations; and a number of the teachers involved in the Seattle University Youth Initiative are alumni of the university. Finally, because of San Diego State University's intentional effort to build a virtuous cycle with the community of City Heights and the relatively long-term implementation of their partnership (in relation to the other institutions in our study), dozens of university graduates have become community partners.

The Importance of Boundaries and Role Clarity

By drawing upon the practices described here, campus and community partners engaged in place-based community engagement can build and maintain strong relationships that lead to long-term success. As we observed in several of our site visits, when working well, the boundaries between campus and community organizations become blurred. Yet blending efforts too much can also lead to trouble. As evidenced by some of the preceding quotes, many community partners voiced the need to clarify roles and responsibilities in order to manage the dynamic and intense nature of the place-based initiatives. This sentiment was echoed by many of the university partners.

For example, one of the leaders of Drexel's Dornsife Center shared with pride how she and her staff worked earnestly to respond to community requests for partnerships and programs. Yet she also noted that "we are not an ATM," indicating that they sought to be clear how Drexel could assist and also where it was unable to respond. Seattle University's close working relationships with local schools has also led to an effort to have clear definitions of roles. For example, although the Seattle University staff and students who work in the local public school buildings have great enthusiasm for various new curricular and educational programs, they recognize that they are guests in the building, serving under the auspices of teachers, school administrators, and parents. For place-based initiatives, blurring lines while maintaining role clarity is another important factor in achieving campus and community impact.

Lessons Learned From Community Partners

The voices and perspectives of community partners are essential to the success of place-based community engagement initiatives, as evidenced in the following key lessons arising from community partners and the process of partnering:

1. *Trust and communication are vital.* When campus and community partners trust each other and communicate frequently, challenges that arise can quickly be addressed. Yet trust among partners takes time and is earned through the process of partnering.
2. *Develop quick feedback loops.* Successful partners often create structures that swiftly surface to address emerging issues.
3. *Remain vigilant about racial and cultural differences.* Often the dominant racial identities of the students and staff of universities engaged in place-based initiatives do not reflect the identities of residents and leaders living in the community. Campus and community leaders must carefully navigate these differences to avoid perpetuating the very problems they are striving to solve.
4. *Draw upon the dynamism of alumni.* The virtuous cycle of alumni from the university working as community partners or as campus leaders of the place-based initiative strengthens partnerships and expands the capacity for positive social change.
5. *Maintain role clarity while blurring the boundaries.* Seeking to fully partner with each other while being attentive to roles and responsibilities strengthens the potential for enduring partnerships.

The lessons, voices of partners, and examples we explore in this chapter are essential for a place-based community engagement initiative to attain success. When leaders from the campus and the community partner together as equals they can achieve significant impact on campus and in the community. But how exactly does one measure the impact of such complex and multifaceted initiatives? In the next chapter, we explore how assessment, evaluation and a focus on outcomes can inform strategy and drive results.

PURSUING RESULTS

The Practice of Assessment and Outcomes

Using data to inform decision-making and measure results is an important aspect of a place-based initiative. Such data are useful in establishing identifiable (and measurable goals) across partners. Utilizing data-based decision-making also allows for clear communication among partners regarding what is and what is not working and, if necessary, ways to improve the process. This allows partners to be accountable and responsive to each other. Having facility with outcomes, assessment, and evaluations also allows an initiative to tell its story to partners and external parties, including potential donors and funders. This can be helpful if an initiative intends to pursue national recognition, which often requires data from assessment, evaluation, or outcomes. Ultimately, the careful use of data, assessment, and evaluation serves as a guide in developing the initiative's strategies and creating accountability for results.

As an initiative develops, so too does its strategy for assessment and outcomes. For the university, context also plays a role in determining what type of information is most useful in informing decision-making. Two aspects of an institution's context that often influence place-based community engagement are its resources and its culture. In this chapter we draw upon examples from the institutions in our study to explore the strategies and practices of assessment and outcomes for place-based community engagement.

Definitions

The higher education and nonprofit sectors use many types of data collection and data analysis and draw upon many concepts and definitions. For this chapter, we will draw upon several common terms and definitions (Patton, 2011; Schuh, Biddix, Dean, & Kinzie, 2016; Yarbrough, Shulha, Hopson, & Caruthers, 2010). These include *outcomes, assessment,* and *evaluation.*

Outcomes are a type of result. In many cases, outcomes are goals that the place-based initiative is pursuing (e.g., a goal of increasing parent participation in an event). Establishing and monitoring outcomes enables a place-based initiative to examine the results from its investment of resources. Identifying and tracking outcomes can be a relatively simple process that does not require specialized expertise or a large investment of resources.

Assessment consists of data-based activities that provide information to improve a process, program, or event (e.g., whether publicizing the event via word of mouth is a good use of staff time). Assessment is most useful when it is designed to address a problem. Assessments can range from simple to complex, with the latter requiring significant time and expertise. There are also cases when it is helpful to employ an external party to complete an assessment, especially if validity or bias is a concern. Some examples of assessment in higher education include measuring participation and assessing needs, satisfaction, or costs (Schuh et al., 2016).

Evaluation focuses on understanding a program or event (e.g., whether the event worked well) by providing a value judgment (e.g., yes or no). An evaluation involves a process of collecting and/or examining data and then issuing a conclusion. Using an evaluation to improve practice is a critical step in the evaluation process (Patton, 2011). For place-based community engagement, using evaluation results can help to determine whether an initiative has influenced an issue or context (e.g., whether the initiative has contributed to the improvement of student learning at a neighborhood school). Similar to assessment, evaluations can be simple or very complicated. More complex evaluations, such as analyzing data across multiple organizations or bringing together multiple datasets, may require advanced expertise and, in some cases, identifying an external evaluator. For some partnerships (e.g., government grants and partnerships with school districts), evaluations are often required and negotiated through a formal partnership agreement.

At the institutional level, context also plays a role in determining what type of information is most useful (or valued) in informing decision-making. Two particular facets of an institution's context that inform its approach to assessment include existing resources (e.g., institutional research staff) and its campus culture of change. For example, a university that has a culture of evaluation may not value outcomes or assessments as much as evaluation. In this chapter, we explore the strategies and practices of assessment and outcomes for place-based community engagement, as these are the tools used most frequently by initiatives.

Strategies and Practices

Reflecting their wide-ranging contexts, institutional strategy and capacity for assessment and monitoring outcomes varied across the five universities we examined. Drexel and Seattle University, although very different types of institutions, presented the most developed strategies for data-driven decision-making. A contributing factor to Drexel and Seattle University's more nuanced strategies might be that both institutions also had a strong record of partnering on government grants and receiving support from donors.

Loyola Maryland and the University of San Diego have more emergent strategies for data-based decision-making. Loyola Maryland recently hired an associate director for administration who oversees operations and assessment and is expanding its internal assessment and outcome capacity. The University of San Diego has historically applied a more organic approach to assessment and has an institutional culture of informal partner-centered processes and engagement with outcomes. San Diego State University presents yet another type of strategy, one that has relied primarily on the interests and resources of its lead funding partner, Price Philanthropies.

Context Matters

The universities in our study span a wide range of institutional types, including private research, public research, and small- and medium-sized private religiously affiliated campuses. The variance in these institutional types has a significant influence on how each institution approaches assessing and monitoring outcomes of its place-based initiative.

The two research institutions in our study, Drexel and San Diego State University, are both classified as doctoral institutions with higher research activity and have significant institutional resources to engage in assessment and evaluation. The institutional research offices at both institutions have at least four full-time staff members, which gives them more capacity to support the evaluation and assessment of their place-based initiatives. The University of San Diego, which is also classified as a doctoral institution but is similar in size to Loyola Maryland and Seattle University, also has more than four staff members in its institutional research office. Classified as master's institutions, Loyola Maryland and Seattle University have fewer staff members in their institutional research units.

As research institutions, Drexel and San Diego State University's campus cultures of assessment are stronger by design. Faculty members at these institutions are more likely to be engaged in resource-intensive research and are likely to have stronger skills and interest in engaging in assessment and evaluation. For example, San Diego State University has a faculty-led statistical modeling group, illustrating both faculty interest and expertise with advanced methods of assessment and evaluation.

This is not to say that faculty at master's institutions do not have strong research training and abilities. Rather, compared with research universities, incentives and resources for faculty involvement in assessment and evaluation at these institutions are more limited. Staff members at Loyola Maryland and Seattle University noted that finding faculty members to partner with on evaluation and assessment efforts was difficult. In fact, both campuses hired internal assessment staff in order to meet their initiatives' demands for assessment and evaluation. In addition, because of limited faculty and university resources, Seattle University has used consultants to address some of its place-based assessment and evaluation needs. For example, on three occasions an external evaluator has conducted developmental evaluations of Seattle University's partnerships in order to identify what is working and what could be strengthened.

Formal Assessment

The place-based initiatives at Drexel, San Diego State University, and Seattle University have strong cultures of formal assessment and evaluation. This might be the result of these initiatives' funding sources and partnerships. All three institutions have partnered on large federal grants and/or have strong partnerships with school districts, two entities that are well known for stringent assessment and evaluation standards.

Federal Grantees

Drexel and Seattle University's place-based initiatives have a strong culture of formal assessments and evaluations, including the most in quantity and in the level of high-quality assessments and evaluations of the institutions we studied. This may be largely attributed to the fact that both are recipients of federal grants through the Promise Neighborhood and Choice Neighborhood initiatives. Both of these federal initiatives require (a) proposals that present a sophisticated strategy and plan for assessment and evaluation and (b) the ability to execute the plan upon receiving the funds.

For example, when Seattle University partnered with the Seattle Housing Authority to pursue the Choice Neighborhood grant, Seattle University developed a detailed metrics matrix utilizing Seattle Public Schools student data that set measurable year-by-year goals for the reading and math progress of children living in the public housing community of Yesler Terrace. Once Seattle Housing Authority received the grant, they contracted with the Seattle University Center for Community Engagement to track actual K–12 student outcomes. Table 8.1 illustrates data points across the K–12 educational pipeline of students.

This matrix provides robust data to understand student progress. Since testing in reading begins in the third grade in the state of Washington, this matrix allows an opportunity to look at data across schools (elementary and middle school), which is helpful in tracking achievement in a P–20 partnership. Examining a row in this matrix horizontally from third to eighth grade illustrates the progress of a particular cohort. Examining this matrix vertically in a column demonstrates the impact of strategies on specific grade-level assessment over time across cohorts (e.g., eighth-grade assessment for cohorts J–O).

Strong Partnerships With School Districts

San Diego State University and Seattle University have strong working partnerships with their local school districts, the San Diego Unified School District and Seattle Public Schools, respectively. Partnerships with school districts often require a lengthy memorandum of understanding (MOU) process that outlines the partnership, including key measurements of data points. At Seattle University, this MOU process included the presentation of major partnership activities and the development of a data-sharing agreement that allows the university to receive academic and nonacademic data indicators in order to track the school success of children in the place-based initiative. This was an extensive process and one that required significant trust and cooperation between the university and its school and district partners. A school district administrator shared,

> I think breaking down some of the barriers, particularly around FERPA (Family Educational Rights and Privacy Act) and data sharing and getting that to work [is important]. . . . I know you need that [K–12 student] data to meet your outcomes. [Seattle University] was really able to create an understanding with the district and break through that so we can really use the university's expertise in data analysis. We created a system together which was more sophisticated than what we had before. The teachers can really manipulate the data and really use that the data on a weekly basis in the classroom.

At San Diego State University, Price Philanthropies played a major role in establishing data metrics and partnering with the school district. Yet San Diego State University's strong institutional culture and resources for research and assessment allowed it to quickly meet the needs of the partnership. For example, when an evaluation was needed, a Price Philanthropies staff member noted, "We send out an RFP [request for proposal] to faculty members and have had them do the evaluations."

TABLE 8.1

Seattle University Choice Neighborhood Grant Sample Matrix

Cohort Label	Grade Level	3rd Grade Reading Assessment		4th Grade Reading Assessment		5th Grade Reading Assessment		6th Grade Reading Assessment		7th Grade Reading Assessment		8th Grade Reading Assessment	
Cohort O	8th											*15/24*	*63%*
Cohort N	7th									*9/17*	*53%*	11/17	65%
Cohort M	6th							*14/29*	*48%*	16/29	55%	17/29	59%
Cohort L	5th					*17/25*	*68%*	19/25	76%	76/25	60%	21/25	84%
Cohort K	4th			*20/34*	*58%*	17/34	65%	18/34	68%	25/34	74%	26/34	77%
Cohort J	3rd	*15/31*	*48%*	18/31	58%	21/31	68%	22/31	71%	23/31	74%	29/31	94%

Source: Seattle University. Used with permission. Washington state annual assessment data. Please note that sample data are presented (not actual student data).

A key San Diego State University faculty partner confirmed the use of RFPs to faculty and observed the benefit of this practice, stating that it enabled faculty to engage in some applied research activity. The faculty member shared, "We have had evaluation work on our partnership, which was completed by a faculty member in our program. It was nice for this faculty member to contribute in this way since his area of expertise is more quantitative and he does not work as closely with the schools." Regardless of the process, partnerships with school districts bring about complex assessment and evaluation requirements and needs. Whether these are internally completed (San Diego State University) or externally completed, or some combination of both (Seattle University), the need for strong expertise and capacity is critical.

Continuous Improvement: Temperature Checks and Logic Models

Data-driven decision-making was used as a continuous improvement strategy for many of the institutions that we studied. A common practice that arose from our research was the use of "temperature checks." At Drexel University, an executive director shared, "We do check-ins with our partners—what is working well, what do we need to address? Checking the temperature of the relationship is important. We want to know of our successes and address problems before they get out of hand." Similarly, at Loyola Maryland, a community partner with Strong City Baltimore spoke about this practice. "We see each other all the time . . . sometimes in meetings at other places in town and [the director] will check in on us. What's working right? What do we need to make right . . . things like that."

Temperature checks can also occur spontaneously. For example, during a site visit to a middle school, the university program administrator engaged in a side conversation with the community partner we were visiting. She asked about some new equipment that had been purchased that she could see kids playing with. The on-site partner noted, "The kids love playing on the new toy. . . . It was worth buying it and waiting for it. [The concerned campus administrator] now even likes it." Later, the administrator admitted how challenging it had been to purchase the playground equipment, but seeing the kids play on it made it worth it. As these examples illustrate, doing temperature checks with partners offers a low-cost way of consistently assessing the partnership and making necessary adjustments.

Loyola Maryland is pursuing another strategy, the use of logic models (W.K. Kellogg Foundation, 2004). As the associate director for administration explained,

A logic model is a pictorial representation of how a program is supposed to work. Unlike a traditional flow chart, a logic model is a "systematic and visual way to present and share your understanding of the relationships among the resources you have to operate your program, the activities you plan, and the changes or results you hope to achieve" (W.K. Kellogg Foundation, 2004).

The new associate director for administration also explained where Loyola's initiative is in their process:

> We are in the process of developing logic models for all of our programs. . . . Each person is putting together a programmatic logical model and then there will be a [complete office] model. In its simplest form, it's about the outcomes, and what we do (programs, events, etc.) to achieve our goals. With a logic model in place, the Center for Community Service and Justice can better track and ensure that its activities have a direct correlation to its goals and desired impact on its students and the community.

The Loyola Maryland director added, "We are excited for what is to come when we implement this [logic model strategy] fully."

"Telling the Story" to Stakeholders

Spending time and resources for assessment and outcomes also enables institutions to "tell the story" of their initiatives to key stakeholders. Although most initiatives can share anecdotal evidence, campuses that effectively draw upon more nuanced data often have a more compelling story to tell. For example, on several occasions, the executive director of the Seattle University Center for Community Engagement has presented to the university's board of trustees as well as the university's fund development campaign committee. Using data such as the academic progress of neighborhood children to tell the story of the Youth Initiative instilled confidence among these groups. Combining vignettes and evaluation results offers an effective strategy to speak to audiences that often seek to understand the larger framework of an initiative and its context within the university.

The executive director of the Dornsife Center for Neighborhood Partnerships at Drexel noted that community partners valued the use of a data-driven approach. She observed, "Community partners want to know that working with us makes a difference. . . . Sharing our evaluations with them helps us do that. They enjoy hearing about how students have grown or learned something new." The senior vice provost of university and community partnerships at Drexel noted that data are also helpful to funders. She said, "You have to be able to illustrate how you can make a difference, using data to show you have made an impact." Thus, using data from assessments and evaluations to tell the place-based initiative's story enhanced the university's messaging to key stakeholders, including funders.

Honors and Awards: President's Honor Role and Carnegie Classification

President's Higher Education Community Service Honor Roll

All of the institutions in our study except San Diego State University applied for and received designation on the President's Higher Education Community Service Honor Roll, a significant institutional honor. Moreover, in the latest honor roll process, the University of San Diego and Seattle University received honor roll designations with "distinction." Through their applications the institutions needed to present outcomes, including estimates when necessary, for student and community engagement as well as economic impact. In addition, the application required extensive data on community partnerships to illustrate influence and impact. Our review of these honor roll applications suggests that institutions that have outcomes data, particularly from more structured evaluations and assessments, are more prepared to apply for and possibly receive recognition.

Carnegie Classification for Community Engagement

All of the institutions in our study have received the Carnegie Classification for Community Engagement, which is viewed as a prominent national honor. This is a voluntary, evidence-based award which recognizes institutions for excellence in community engagement work, including multiple questions focusing on strategy, process, and outcomes (see Figure 8.1). In looking deeper at the 2015 applications (new and renewal) a number of questions sought out community-focused information, specifically on the foundational indicators, institutional commitment, and outreach sections (Carnegie Foundation for the Advancement of Teaching, n.d.).

Taken together, the President's Honor Roll and Carnegie Classification opportunities demonstrate that investing in a place-based initiative's capacity and infrastructure for outcomes and assessment offers many benefits and can facilitate national recognition.

Figure 8.1. Carnegie Classification for Community Engagement community-focused questions.

FOUNDATIONAL INDICATORS
Question 3a: Does the institution have mechanisms for systematic assessment of community perceptions of the institution's engagement with community? Describe the mechanisms for systematic assessment.
Question 3b: Does the institution aggregate and use all of its assessment data related to community engagement? Describe how the data are used.
INSTITUTIONAL COMMITMENT
Question 2d: Does the institution invest its financial resources in the community for the purposes of community engagement and community development?
Question 3a: Does the institution maintain systematic campus-wide tracking or documentation mechanisms to record and/or track engagement with the community? Describe systematic campus-wide tracking or documentation mechanisms.
Question 3b: Does the institution use the data from those mechanisms? Describe how the institution uses the data from those mechanisms.
Question 4d: If yes (*Question 4a:* Are there systemic campus-wide mechanisms to measure the impact of institutional engagement?), indicate the focus of these systematic campus-wide assessment mechanisms and describe one key finding for Impact on Community.
Question 4f: Does the institution use the data from the assessment mechanisms?
Question 7: Does the institution have a "voice" or role for impact on institutional or department planning for community engagement?
OUTREACH AND PARTNERSHIPS
Question 4a: Does the institution or departments promote attention to the mutuality and reciprocity of the partnerships? Describe the strategies for promoting attention to the mutuality and reciprocity of partnerships.
Question 4b: If yes, describe the mechanisms and how the data have been used to improve reciprocity and mutual benefit.

Lessons Learned From Assessment and Outcomes

Careful use of assessment, evaluation, and outcomes can significantly enhance place-based community engagement initiatives. In the following we present five central lessons arising from the institutions we studied.

1. *Context matters.* Like many aspects of pursuing a place-based initiative, the university's size, focus, resources, institutional culture, funders, and Carnegie Classification often significantly inform the approach to assessment and outcomes.

2. *Assessment can drive continuous improvement.* The long-term nature of a place-based initiative invites a long-term approach to assessment that emphasizes continuous improvement.

3. *Strong partnerships can positively influence assessment.* Trusting campus and community partnerships contributes to the development of logic models and also assists in making programmatic changes in real time.

4. *Draw upon assessment to tell the story.* Thoughtfully designed assessment processes and tools can provide valuable information to tell the story of the place-based initiative to campus and community partners as well as funders.

5. *Assessment can build the case for national recognition and federal grant applications.* Carefully tracking input and outcome data provides evidence to include in national community engagement award applications. Such thoughtful attention to assessment can increase an institution's ability to seek federal, state, and assessment-heavy foundation grants, which increases the likelihood of receiving recognition.

Assessment, evaluation, and outcomes provide tools and processes that fuel success. By strategically drawing upon the lessons and examples presented in this chapter, campus and community partners can maximize the potential of attaining positive results.

LESSONS LEARNED AND
MOVING FORWARD

Throughout this book we've sought to provide an overview of the process and practice of pursuing a place-based community engagement strategy within the context of institutions of higher education. From our research and analysis, we believe that place-based community engagement can lead to positive transformation within our universities and within our local communities. From the theoretical to the practical, our explorations have surfaced many lessons and promising practices. Through this project we have also seen the many challenges arising from a place-based approach. As we come to an end of this exploration, we also are keenly aware of numerous remaining questions that, if examined with depth and rigor, can expand the influence and impact of place-based community engagement on our campuses and in our communities.

In chapter 2, we presented five key principles of place-based community engagement:

1. A geographic focus
2. Equal emphasis on campus and community impact
3. Long-term vision and commitment
4. University-wide engagement that animates the mission and develops the institution
5. Drawing upon the concept of collective impact

In this final chapter, we return to these principles in order to synthesize what we have learned, identify some remaining challenges, and pose questions for further exploration.

A Geographic Focus

Through place-based community engagement, colleges and universities concentrate their partnerships and programs on a well-defined geographic area. These areas may have some existing organization or established neighborhood boundaries. Yet, as the institutions in our study illustrate, the geographic area of focus is often socially constructed by the university. This focus on place departs from the dominant community engagement approach utilized by most universities and colleges in the United States. By focusing on place, the university becomes more declarative of its external goals and centralizes a geographic area and the people who live there.

Lessons of Place

As the institutions in our study highlight, the intensive emphasis on "a place" invites the university to deeply understand the historical and current context of its community. By concentrating on a geographic area, each of the universities we visited illustrate how a campus can move beyond seeking partnerships only with individual organizations; rather, many individuals and entities within the neighborhood can potentially become a part of the partnership process. Centering place also provides the institution with a constant reminder to focus on building community capacity and mutually beneficial community-based ideas instead of getting overly focused on university-generated projects or concepts.

The higher education institutions in our study also show us that a focus on place offers faculty a chance to provide rich and innovative clinical experiences in deep and meaningful ways for students and community members, including opportunities for students to learn from community members in the classroom, such as Drexel's Side-by-Side courses. In addition, the place-based focus allows many community partners and university staff to give back and contribute to the communities that they were raised in or engaged with as college or graduate students—creating a powerful cycle of civic engagement. In short, a place-based emphasis increases the likelihood for authentic and trusting campus-community partnerships to develop and expand in order to attain meaningful community engagement and campus impact.

Challenges of Place

Universities focusing their community engagement efforts on one geographic area also face some significant challenges. As noted in chapter 4, one initial challenge experienced during the exploration phase is simply deciding what "place" to focus on and then navigating the campus and community politics of concentrating efforts on this geographic area over the many compelling opportunities to partner in other places and spaces. Another challenge we explored in chapter 6—that all of the institutions we studied have or will likely contend with—is gentrification. Universities must remain attentive to how best to interrupt or mitigate external gentrifying forces and also how to avoid becoming a contributor to gentrification.

For universities who partner with public schools, a long-term challenge emerges with shifting attendance boundaries, whether the result of school district policy, the emergence of charter schools, or specialized programs that draw students from a wider geographic span of the district. Another ever-present challenge is that neighborhoods and universities operate within a much larger economic, political, and social system. Focusing intensely on a geographic area without considering these larger systems may limit long-term success. Finally, the growth of university courses and degrees in online and global modalities (e.g., engaging students outside of a region and online) creates challenges in focusing a university's community engagement on neighborhoods near the "brick-and-mortar" campus.

Remaining Questions About Place

In considering the focus on a geographic area, several remaining questions are worth further exploration:

- Although place-based engagement and an anchor institution strategy are not one and the same, how might an institution that is pursuing place-based community engagement draw upon the research and knowledge arising from anchor institution frameworks? Might place-based engagement be a gateway into institutions seeing themselves as anchors?
- Some institutions have initiatives in areas geographically adjacent to the university (e.g., Drexel, Loyola Maryland, Seattle University, and the University of San Diego), whereas other institutions have nonadjacent initiative locations (e.g., San Diego State University). How does proximity to campus impact an initiative?
- Our study examined five predominantly White institutions in large metropolitan areas of the United States. Does place-based community engagement in higher education look different in rural areas? What does place-based work look like among minority-serving institutions?
- Our study focused on four-year institutions that recruit students nationally and internationally. Might community colleges, which rely on local enrollment, be well suited to engage in place-based community

engagement? Or are they already naturally doing this work because of their focus on a geographic catchment area?

• Does place-based engagement privilege communities that are in close proximity to institutions of higher education? What might be done for communities that do not have a university in their area?

Equal Emphasis on Campus and Community Impact

Most university community engagement programs concentrate the vast majority of their efforts on impacting college student learning or generating new knowledge, and the community engagement offices in our study were similarly situated prior to their place-based initiatives. Because of this bias toward impacting campus, most university community engagement efforts— although there may be some short-term benefits to the community—actually have a limited long-term impact on the community. Perhaps the most powerful aspect of utilizing a place-based community engagement strategy is how it can move the university to focus equally on campus and community impact. What we call the "50-50 proposition" provides immense benefits but also raises new and interesting challenges.

Lessons of the 50-50 Proposition

Focusing evenly on campus and community impact can lead the community to view the university as a much more significant agent of positive change. As we saw with San Diego State University and Price Philanthropies as well as Seattle University and the Seattle Housing Authority, viewing how serious the university is about community impact may lead community partners, government agencies, and funders to ask the university to deepen and expand projects.

In some instances, as we observed at Drexel and Seattle University, this can lead to the expansion of university programs and financial resources that support community engagement. Moving toward a 50-50 proposition can also bring more intellectual, human, and organizational capital to address significant community issues, increasing the potential for identifying solutions. Moreover, as we noted in chapter 6, when there is growth in campus and community partnerships, opportunities for college students to learn and grow their civic leadership capacity can increase.

Adding an externally facing staff member as part of the 50-50 proposition, something that most of the institutions in our study did, can also significantly strengthen the university's reputation with community partners. In addition to clearer communication loops between the university and community partners, the investment of such an asset provides enhanced credibility, which is important for long-term work with and for the community. Finally, in focusing on off-campus issues, externally facing staff will naturally help facilitate the institution's move toward a greater focus on community impact.

Challenges of the 50-50 Proposition

Equally emphasizing campus and community impact also brings new challenges. A greater emphasis on community impact means that the university will need to become more accountable to external partners, external events, and external measurements of success. As the community's issues become the campus's issues, the university may need to become more involved in advocacy related to neighborhood issues. Moreover, because of closer partnerships, the feedback loops between campus and community will increase in speed and intensity, and the need to address issues quickly and thoughtfully will intensify. All of this can complicate how universities operate and call for adjustments to systems and practices. Some campuses that have well-established government and community relations offices and expertise within their current roles (e.g., Loyola Maryland and the University of San Diego) will be well equipped to address challenges that arise in this area. However, most community engagement offices with their current structures and resources lack capacity in this area. This will test the bandwidth of university leaders to understand and respond to community issues.

The 50-50 proposition can also call into question how university community engagement offices go about their work. As detailed in prior chapters, shifting more toward community impact may call for revising job descriptions and restructuring the office. Equally emphasizing campus and community impact also builds in ongoing tension between staff and faculty who focus more on campus impact and others who concentrate more on the community. How campuses embrace and manage this polarity will likely determine the long-term success of their place-based strategies.

An additional central challenge arising from the 50-50 proposition is how campuses, namely historically White institutions, deepen and expand their capacity to address historic and current issues of racism. The field of community engagement in higher education as a whole is led and staffed mostly by White people. Opportunities for all staff members, especially White staff members, to better understand issues of race and equity are limited. In addition, in some circles there is resistance to exploring these issues at all.

All of the place-based efforts in our study involve historically White institutions partnering with racially and culturally diverse communities, providing insight into the many opportunities and challenges of navigating across issues of power and privilege. Through our site visits and conversations, we witnessed how each institution was addressing this challenge, including (a) significantly expanding staff development on topics of race and racism, (b) enhancing the training and preparation of college students serving in the initiative with a particular emphasis on race and the historical contexts of the neighborhood, (c) recruiting and hiring more staff and Students of Color to work in the initiatives, and (d) developing new strategies to incorporate community voice. Although seeing progress, all of the institutions also recognized how much further they needed to go in order to truly address the challenge of taking their 50-50 proposition seriously.

One final challenge to the 50-50 proposition is that national awards and incentives, such as the two we discussed in chapter 8, do not focus equally on campus and community impact. The Carnegie Classification for Community Engagement, one of the most widely recognized hallmarks of a university's commitment to community engagement, places minimal emphasis on community impact, especially for institutions who are renewing their classifications. Although they have asked a number of questions that centered on the community partnership and community outcomes (see chapter 8), only a few questions from the most recent Carnegie application included questions related to community impact. Moreover, the President's Community Service Honor Roll measures community impact as input data, such as the number of books read to a child and the number of garbage bags picked up during a neighborhood clean-up. Although well intentioned, this approach falls short of positioning the community as an equal partner and taking the possible impact of the university more seriously. Without a shift in how national awards and classifications view community impact, the catalyzing effect of the place-based approach may be muted.

Remaining Questions About the 50-50 Proposition

In considering the 50-50 proposition, remaining questions worth further exploration include the following:

- How might place-based initiatives build upon the idea of the "virtuous cycle" that we noted in chapter 6 to bring more and more community members into the leadership of their place-based initiatives?
- Will place-based initiatives, with their equal emphasis on campus and community impact, lead to significant innovations in university

structures and systems? Might these innovations lead to unexpected benefits for universities in terms of new relationships with funders and government institutions and new degree programs?

- What are the attributes of a "highly qualified" staff member in place-based community engagement? Is there a higher degree of multicultural competency and development of one's own identity needed to effectively do this work?

- How do we hold community engagement staff members accountable for doing their own work in the face of issues of systemic power and privilege and their own intersecting identities? And how do we address staff members who are resistant to doing their own work?

- Do the issues of power, privilege, and racism arising from the 50-50 proposition lead campuses to better connect their community engagement strategies with their diversity and inclusion work? What are the promising practices in exploring these linkages? Which specific practices work and which have no impact?

- A final, more existential, consideration is whether the 50-50 proposition is aspirational or attainable. Is it realistic to think that a university, with its predominant constituents of faculty and students, might ever truly achieve an equal impact on its community and campus?

Long-Term Vision and Commitment

Significant change on campus and in the community can take many years of focused and strategic partnerships. This slow and important process calls for a long-term vision and sustained commitment. All of the institutions that we studied demonstrated this commitment. For example, none of the institutions have an end date to their initiatives. The stability created by this long-term commitment creates a foundation for transformation.

Lessons of Long-Term Vision and Commitment

Bill Gates (1995) has famously noted that "We often overestimate what we can do in a year and underestimate what we can do in 10 years." This observation rings true for place-based community engagement; as illustrated by San Diego State University and Seattle University, the longer the duration of the place-based approach, the greater the potential for impact. The gift of this long view is that it invites more of a methodical and systematic approach to pursuing the place-based vision, which can result in much more durable partnerships, programs, funding sources, and leadership.

A common characteristic of each of the institutions in our study is the boldness of their place-based vision. Each institution presented an expansive plan to thoroughly connect its campus and community through comprehensive programs and partnerships. In several cases, presidents challenged their institutions to become the top university in the country for community engagement. Although harboring audacious visions, the institutions in our study also demonstrated a sense of humility and groundedness, particularly in carefully listening to community leaders and residents and thoughtfully designing partnerships that build the capacity of the community.

Challenges of Long-Term Vision and Commitment

Although pursuing an expansive vision through a long-term commitment can lead to significant success, it also can create several distinct challenges. The very nature of a long-term or permanent commitment means that change and disruption will naturally occur. In chapter 6 we noted how transitions in a university president, a key staff member, or a major community partner can threaten a place-based initiative. Ensuring that leaders at many levels of the institution and community own the place-based vision will likely limit the negative effect of any one person's departure or transition.

The disruptive forces that are impacting many universities' business models can challenge an institution's long-term commitment to place-based community engagement. When budgets become tight, questions will arise about how to best invest the institution's finite financial resources. Some may question the use of university resources to support place-based engagement. Creating a business argument for place-based community engagement may buffer this potential critique. Many of the leaders from the institutions we studied noted that their place-based initiatives presented the institutions with new funding opportunities and led to greater local and national visibility. For both San Diego State University and Seattle University, the place-based initiative led to scholarship funding to attract neighborhood students to the institution. Moreover, a recent study found that students involved in community engagement during college found higher-paying initial jobs after college compared to students not involved in the community (Matthews, Dorfman, & Wu, 2015). Place-based community engagement can impact both the institutions' and college students' bottom lines.

Even when gentrification is not present, few geographic areas remain static. Neighborhoods and communities will continue to evolve, which will test institutions' long-term vision and commitment to place-based engagement. Although certainly not the preferred approach, changes in neighborhoods and communities may lead a university to alter the geographic focus of its place-based approach.

Remaining Questions About Long-Term Vision and Commitment

The following are among the questions needing further examination:

- How essential to the success of the place-based endeavor is support from the university president? When a president who championed a place-based strategy leaves the institution, can a place-based initiative continue to thrive? Conversely, when a new president begins at the institution, can the structure and design of the place-based approach allow for further scaling up of the initiative? Our study of five institutions might be too limited a sample to fully answer these questions.
- Could a business argument for place-based community engagement influence campus leaders and donors who are not swayed by the moral arguments arising from the strategy? Conversely, in presenting a business case is there a risk of losing credibility or instilling cynicism among some community and campus partners?
- How best do institutions evaluate the need to adjust or change the geographic boundaries of their place-based initiatives? Who needs to be involved in this assessment and who actually makes the decision?

University-Wide Engagement That Animates the Mission and Develops the Institution

A place-based initiative can increase its likelihood of success by comprehensively engaging multiple units of the university in partnerships and programs. Catalyzing numerous departments and divisions through a unified geographic focus brings valuable additional resources to the wider community and also can deepen university students' learning and faculty research. The institutions we studied all engaged multiple departments and schools in their place-based work and, as highlighted in previous chapters, several developed their strategic plans around place-based engagement strategies.

Lessons of University-Wide Engagement

As we explored in prior chapters, the university president often provides the spark and consistent executive leadership for a place-based initiative to develop. Yet initiatives that are solely dependent on the president are unlikely to reach their full potential and may face risks once the president leaves office.

As we observed from the institutions we studied, involving other members of the university community, from students to faculty to staff, creates a more expansive platform of partnerships and programs. Consistently inviting faculty to learn about the initiative through creative programming, like Seattle University's local community immersions, fuels curricular innovation and can lead to permanent connections to academic programs. As we discussed more extensively in chapter 6, the creative involvement of students through new academic opportunities (courses, certificates, minors, etc.) and cocurricular projects deepens student learning and provides energy to the partnerships. In some cases, as we saw with Loyola Maryland, a faculty member may take on a new leadership role. Strategically including trustees and funders can also lead to stronger institutional ownership and greater financial support for the initiative.

One of the notable aspects of a university is the sheer expansiveness of departments and resources that could be connected to the community to build the capacity of local organizations, residents, and leaders, especially when integrated into strategic plans like many of the campuses in our study. With programs in business, education, health, law, social work, and many other disciplines, as the institutions in our study illuminate, universities possess countless opportunities to link courses, clinical experiences, research projects, and other experiential learning opportunities to their local communities. Although pursuing different strategies and approaches, all of the institutions we studied leveraged some campus academic departments to pursue community benefits.

Place-based community engagement, as evidenced by Drexel and the University of San Diego, also can offer universities a thematic platform for their institutions' strategic plans and fund development campaigns. In addition, although most colleges and universities highlight their community engagement efforts in some form, universities pursuing place-based efforts (e.g., Drexel, Seattle University, and the University of San Diego) may further leverage their commitment through marketing and messaging in order to increase their visibility and positive public perception.

As described in previous chapters, place-based community engagement presents potential funders with an expansive invitation to invest in the campus and community. In some cases, funders that have had no prior interest in supporting the university become intrigued by the boldness and focused nature of the university's strategy. Pursuing comprehensive university engagement in one geographic area can spark the interest and imagination of funders and lead to significant additional financial investments.

Challenges of University-Wide Engagement

Striving to fully involve the university in a place-based engagement strategy, although bringing many positive benefits, can also bring challenges. Multiple campus departments pursuing collaboration with community organizations can create confusion for the partners. For example, when a university-affiliated person makes a mistake in a partnership, which is bound to happen, the partner organization may not see the distinction between the individual's actions and those of the entire university; essentially, individual actions can implicate the entire institution. Moreover, with so many campus units engaging in the place-based effort, questions of risk and liability also will likely arise, as we noted in chapter 5. Because the institutions we studied identified one office and/or individual to take the lead on campus-community partnerships, thoughtful communication between this entity and other campus units can mitigate the challenges of confusing partners or damaging university-community relationships.

Utilizing the place-based engagement initiative to share the story of the university's commitment to the community and to enhance visibility and enrollment can present a shadow side. Overplaying or overemphasizing the initiative can potentially produce cynicism among all stakeholders. Another related challenge is the difficulty of authentically representing the university as a partner to and not a savior of the neighborhood. In fact, as we shared in chapter 5, some of the campuses we visited have intentionally recentered their service model to minimize charity-based work that does not have mutuality with the community. Without careful consideration of when and how to message the initiative, university and community members may become skeptical of the university's intentions, questioning whether the place-based initiative is simply a way to make the university look good.

Cynicism and lack of longevity can also arise if the university does not dedicate resources or create policies that incentivize and reward faculty, staff, and students for engaging with the place-based initiative. For example, several of the institutions in our study shared that they provided occasional course buyouts for faculty to take on a leadership or research role. Most of the institutions offered work-study or scholarship opportunities for university students to deepen their involvement. Some of the institutions in our study also offered "release time" for staff to volunteer. Yet none of the universities systematically included community engagement as part of their performance and review structure. For many tenure-track faculty members, this poses a major challenge for engagement, as developing a project with a place-based initiative often requires significant community-focused time that is not often valued or credited for tenure and promotion in a significant way.

Although having the full support of university leadership can facilitate powerful partnerships and generate results, it can also create frustration among members of the university who have other priorities and/or other initiatives that require attention. In addition, marshalling significant university resources to pursue positive community impact may lead some university leaders to question whether assets are being taken away from university students and faculty. At least one of the universities in our study expressed a concern that, if not managed carefully, its initiative could "swamp the university." Although no easy answer exists, leaders of place-based initiatives must remain consistently aware of the internal politics of pursuing a university-wide effort. Staying focused on how university involvement in a place-based effort advances the university's goals of student learning, teaching, and research will help mitigate tensions.

Remaining Questions About University-Wide Involvement

Additional questions to explore include the following:

- What systems and structures for managing full-scale university involvement work best? What are the optimal university structures that encourage involvement but also invite a shared sense of responsibility for community partnerships? Does too much emphasis on involving many campus units lead to a significant number of superficial partnerships with limited depth?
- How best can university marketing and communication efforts balance the opportunity to share the powerful story of university-wide engagement in the place-based effort while being attentive to the potential of cynicism to grow? How best can the university message the importance of the initiative as well as its other many priorities?
- How are institutions pursuing place-based community engagement modifying their faculty rewards and tenure and promotion systems to emphasize community engagement? What are promising strategies to pursue this effort?
- Do national accreditation bodies place any added value on the wide-scale involvement of the university in a place-based initiative? Is there an opportunity to utilize the accreditation system to encourage more expansive university engagement?
- What are the best practices in managing the critique that place-based engagement takes away resources from the campus? Is there a resource scarcity or does the place-based approach expand the pool of resources?

Drawing Upon the Concept of Collective Impact

Throughout our study we have noted the ways that universities can provide direct service or specific resources to community partners. All of the universities in our study mobilized their students to serve in their place-based initiatives in roles such as tutors and mentors. Although these direct service efforts are notable, the true power and impact of the place-based approach is what happens when the university becomes more deeply enmeshed with community partners in pursuing a common goal.

Lessons of Collective Impact

All of the universities that we studied utilized collective impact within their place-based initiatives. In several cases (Drexel and Seattle University) the university served as the backbone of the collective impact effort, whereas in other cases (Loyola Maryland and the University of San Diego) the university seemed to be moving in that direction. For institutions serving as the backbone, the expanded role of convener, such as with Seattle University, provided another powerful way for the university to partner to pursue community impact. Fully utilizing collective impact enabled the institutions we examined to think more like a neighborhood than an individual entity. This naturally leads to focusing more on neighborhood residents and actual neighborhood indicators over organizational needs and measurements. The universities within our study that utilized collective impact also benefited from additional external funding support.

Challenges of Collective Impact

Collective impact can benefit a place-based initiative, but it also can bring forth some unanticipated challenges. The very nature of collective impact calls for organizations to downplay self-interest in the name of collaborating for a universal goal. This can stretch the sense of autonomy of the university and its partner organizations. Another challenge is that most funders want individual organizations to attain specific results; collective impact blurs the lines of organizational leadership and the ability to attribute impact to any one organization or partner. Still another challenge is the risk that the backbone organization, whether the university or another organization, does not act as a neutral convener. This can be a particularly pronounced challenge when the backbone organization is also the funder.

The varying levels of data competency among collective impact collaborators also can create challenges, as some partners may want to significantly emphasize data collection and analysis and others may have little interest or capacity to do so. Another related challenge is that the collective impact partners, because of their various funding strands and organizational affiliations, are most likely being asked to track and analyze metrics that may have little to do with the place-based collective impact strategy. Moreover, as we highlighted in chapter 8, developing data-sharing agreements among multiple organizations can prove challenging. Despite these many obstacles, the universities that we studied valued the collective impact strategy and utilized it as a way of pursuing positive community impact.

Remaining Questions About Collective Impact

Several enduring questions about the use of collective impact within a place-based community engagement initiative include the following:

- What are the strategies to evaluate place-based initiatives that utilize collective impact, particularly when the university plays a convener role? Will funders see the university's role as convener worthy of investment?
- If the convener of the collective impact strategy is the university or a funder, does the power imbalance with smaller organizations in the collaborative negatively impact shared decision-making and resource allocation?
- What role might the university play in building out the data competencies of its partners? Are there particular strategies and activities that work well in building this data infrastructure?
- How do the university and its community partners balance their need for autonomy with collective impact's focus on working as a collaborative?
- None of the institutions in our study included another institution of higher education in its collective impact strategy. Why is this and how might multiple institutions of higher education partner together on a place-based effort? More specifically, what role might community colleges play in uniting with four-year universities and colleges?
- What additional partners could be invited to join the place-based collective impact strategy? For example, high-tech companies are pursuing innovative ideas and strategies and also generating tremendous wealth and yet, at least from our study, have limited connection to place-based initiatives.

Conclusion

"When the heart is touched by direct experience the mind may be challenged to change" (Kolvenbach, 2000). This quote, from the former worldwide leader of the Jesuits, Rev. Peter Hans Kolvenbach, S.J., appears in big, bold print along the entire office wall of the Seattle University Center for

Community Engagement. For years Seattle University has drawn upon this quote as inspiration for connecting faculty and students to community issues. In many ways, the quote makes visible what we often take for granted; we learn from and are changed by our experiences. For almost 50 years this idea has undergirded the field of community engagement in higher education.

Yet what if we think of this quote in a more expansive manner? What if the hearts of our institutions, particularly our universities, were impacted through their direct experiences with those residing in their local neighborhoods? What if our universities as entire institutions challenged themselves to think differently about their place in their communities and the impact they could have on their neighborhoods?

Throughout this book we have presented one strategy for how universities can more fully embody their potential of educating their students; conducting compelling academic research; and positively impacting residents or their community, particularly those residents experiencing marginalization because of issues of race, class, and immigration status. By pursuing a place-based approach, universities and their community partners have a chance to pursue expansive long-term partnerships that may profoundly impact the campus and community. In fully embracing the place-based framework, the boundaries between campus and community become blurred and new possibilities emerge. Amid this process, our society can find new innovations and a chance to more fully live out our beliefs in a more just and compassionate world.

REFERENCES

Astin, A. W., Vogelgesang, L. J., Ikeda, E. K., & Yee, J. A. (2000). *How service-learning affects students*. Los Angeles, CA: UCLA Higher Education Research Institute.

Bailey, T. R., Jaggars, S. S., & Jenkins, D. (2015). *Redesigning America's community colleges: A clearer path to student success*. Cambridge, MA: Harvard University Press.

Balk, G. (2017, June 12). The rise and dramatic fall of King County's black homeowners. *The Seattle Times*. Retrieved from http://www.seattletimes.com/seattle-news/data/the-rise-and-dramatic-fall-of-king-countys-black-homeowners/

Baxter, P., & Jack, S. (2008). Qualitative case study methodology: Study design and implementation for novice researchers. *The Qualitative Report, 13*(4), 544–559. Retrieved from http://nsuworks.nova.edu/tqr/vol13/iss4/2

Bayside Community Center. (n.d.). *About Bayside*. Retrieved from http://www.baysidecc.org/about-bayside/

Beason, T. (2016, January 14). As Seattle grapples with growth, a question: Whose city is it? *The Seattle Times*, PNW Northwest Magazine, Northwest Living Section.

Broader, Bolder Approach to Education (BBA). (n.d.). *Partners for Education at Berea College, Berea, Kentucky*. Retrieved from http://www.boldapproach.org/case-study/partners-for-education-at-berea-college-berea-kentucky/

Burks, M. (2014, November 18). San Diego's richest poor neighborhood, twenty years later. *Voices of San Diego*. Retrieved from http://www.voiceofsandiego.org/neighborhood-growth/san-diegos-richest-poor-neighborhood-two-decades-later/

Burns, T., & Brown, B. (2012). *Final report: Lessons from a national scan of comprehensive place-based philanthropic initiatives*. Pittsburgh, PA: The Urban Ventures, Heinz Endowments. Retrieved from http://www.heinz.org/UserFiles/File/Place-Based/UrbanVentures_final-report.pdf

Butin, D. (2006). The limits of service-learning in higher education. *The Review of Higher Education, 29*(4), 473–498.

Carnegie Foundation for the Advancement of Teaching. (n.d.). *Carnegie elective community engagement classification first time classification documentation framework*. Boston, MA: New England Resource for Higher Education. Retrieved from http://nerche.org/images/stories/projects/Carnegie/2015/2015_first-time_framework.pdf

City of San Diego. (n.d.). *Linda Vista*. Retrieved from https://www.sandiego.gov/citycouncil/cd7/neighborhoods/lindavista

Consensus Organizing Center. (n.d.). *Mission statement.* Retrieved from http://consensus.sdsu.edu/

Craig, R. (2015). *College disrupted: The great unbundling of higher education.* New York, NY: Palgrave.

Creswell, J. W. (2013). *Qualitative inquiry and research design: Choosing among five approaches* (3rd ed.). Washington DC: Sage.

Crime in Philadelphia—Mantua. (n.d.). *Philadelphia Inquirer.* Retrieved from http://data.inquirer.com/crime/neighborhood/mantua

Crow, M. W., & Dabars, W. B. (2015). *Designing the new American university.* Baltimore, MD: Johns Hopkins University Press.

Drexel University. (n.d.a). *About Drexel University.* Retrieved from http://drexel.edu/about/history/

Drexel University. (n.d.b). *Saxby's coffee co-op.* Retrieved from http://drexel.edu/difference/co-op/saxbys/

Drexel University Dornsife Center for Neighborhood Partnerships. (n.d.). *Arts and culture.* Retrieved from http://drexel.edu/dornsifecenter/programs/arts-and-culture/

Drexel University Human Resources. (n.d.) *Home Purchase Assistance Program.* Retrieved from http://drexel.edu/hr/benefits/voluntary/homepurchase/

Drexel University Lindy Center for Civic Engagement. (n.d.). *Community based learning courses.* Retrieved from http://drexel.edu/lindycenter/students/courses/community-based-learning/

Drexel University Office of the President. (n.d.). *Biography.* Retrieved from http://drexel.edu/president/JohnFry/biography/

Drexel University Office of University and Community Partnerships. (n.d.a). *Civic engagement.* Retrieved from http://drexel.edu/civicengagement/

Drexel University Office of University and Community Partnerships. (n.d.b). *Drexel University neighborhood initiatives.* Retrieved from http://drexel.edu/civicengagement/neighborhood/overview/

DrexelNOW. (n.d.). *Drexel's School of Public Health receives transformative $45 million gift from Dana and David Dornslife.* Retrieved from http://drexel.edu/now/archive/2015/September/School-of-Public-Health-Naming/

Dubb, S., McKinley, S., & Howard, T. (2013, August). *The anchor dashboard: Aligning institutional practice to meet low-income community needs.* Takoma Park, MD: The University of Maryland Democracy Collaborative.

Erickson, J., & Anderson, J. B. (Eds.). (1997). *Learning with the community: Concepts and models for service-learning in teacher education.* Sterling, VA: Stylus.

Eyler, J., & Giles, D.E. Jr. (1999). *Where's the learning in service-learning?* San Francisco, CA: Jossey Bass.

Feister, L. (2011). *Measuring change while changing measures: Learning in and from the evaluation of making connections.* Baltimore, MD: Annie E. Casey Foundation. Retrieved from http://www.aecf.org/m/resourcedoc/aecf-MeasuringChangeWhileChangingMeasures-2011.pdf

Fry, J. A. (2010). *Drexel University convocation speech.* Retrieved from http://drexel.edu/president/messages/speeches/2010/October/convocation-2010/

Furco, A. (1999). *Self-assessment rubric for institutionalizing service learning in higher education.* Berkeley, CA: UC Berkeley Service-Learning Research and Development Center.

Gates, B. (1995). *The road ahead.* New York, NY: Viking Press.

Goldrick-Rab, S. (2016). *Paying the price: College costs, financial aid, and the betrayal of the American dream.* Chicago, IL: University of Chicago Press.

Guajardo, M. A., Guajardo, F., Janson, C., & Militello, M. (2016). *Reframing community partnerships in education: Uniting the power of place and the wisdom of people.* New York, NY: Routledge.

Hardin, M. C., Eribes, R., & Poster, C. (Eds.). (2006). *From the studio to the streets: Service-learning in planning and architecture.* Sterling, VA: Stylus.

Harlem Children's Zone. (n.d.). *History—The beginning of the Children's Zone.* Retrieved from http://hcz.org/about-us/history/

Harris, J. T., III. (2016). *The University of San Diego convocation speech.* Retrieved from https://www.sandiego.edu/president/writings-addresses/fall-convocation-2016 .php

Harris, J. T., III, & Pickron-Davis, M. (2013). From gates to engagement: A ten-year retrospective of Widener University's journey to reclaim its soul and fulfill its mission as a leading metropolitan university. *Journal of Higher Education Outreach and Engagement, 17*(3), 47–67.

Hartley, M., & Saltmarsh, J. (2016). A brief history of a movement and American higher education. In M. Post, E. Ward, N.V. Longo, & J. Saltmarsh (Eds.), *Next-generation engagement and the future of higher education: Publicly engaged scholars* (pp. 34–60). Sterling, VA: Stylus.

Healthy Communities Assessment Tool. (n.d.). *San Diego, California—Neighborhood rankings.* Retrieved from http://hci-sandiego.sandag.org/neighborhood-ranking

Heffernan, K. (2001). *Fundamentals of service-learning course construction.* Providence, RI: Rhode Island Campus Compact.

Henderson, B. (2016, September 20). *Why is Seattle so racially segregated?* Retrieved from http://kuow.org/post/why-seattle-so-racially-segregated

Hodges, R. A., & Dubb, S. (2012). *The road half traveled: University engagement at a crossroads.* East Lansing, MI: Michigan State University Press.

Holland, B. (1997). Analyzing institutional commitment to service: A model of key organizational factors. *Michigan Journal of Community Service-Learning, 4*(1), 30–41.

Institute for Educational Leadership. (2015). *Coalition for Community Schools.* Retrieved from www.communityschools.org

Jennewein, C. (2014, October 28). Couple gives $3 million for community and social action center. *Times of San Diego.* Retrieved from http://timesofsandiego .com/education/2014/10/28/bay-area-couple-makes-transformative-3-million-gift-usd/

Kania, J., & Kramer, M. (2011, Winter). Collective impact. *Stanford Social Innovation Review, 9*(1).

Karp, M. M., & Klempin, S. (2016). *Improving student services for military veterans.* New York, NY: Columbia University, Teachers College, Community College Research Center.

Kelly, A. P., Howell, J. S., & Sattin-Bajaj, C. (Eds.). (2016). *Matching students to opportunity: Expanding college choice, access, and quality.* Boston, MA: Harvard University Press.

Kim, P. B. (2015, July 10). Map: Legacy of segregation lingers in Baltimore. *The Baltimore Sun.*

Knight, M. G., & Maricano, J. E. (2013). *College ready: Preparing Black and Latina/o youth for higher education—A culturally relevant approach.* New York, NY: Teachers College Press.

Kolvenbach, Peter Hans. (2000, October). *The service of faith and the promotion of justice in American Jesuit higher education.* Speech delivered at Commitment to Justice in Jesuit Higher Education Conference, Santa Clara University, Santa Clara, CA. Retrieved from https://www.scu.edu/ic/programs/ignatian-tradition-offerings/stories/the-service-of-faith-and-the-promotion-of-justice-in-american-jesuit-higher-education.html

Koth, K. (2013). A neighborhood partnership: A model for transformative justice. *Conversations on Jesuit Higher Education, 44*(22), 335.

Lewin, T. (2012, February 4). Taking more seats on campus: Foreigners also pay the freight. *The New York Times.* Retrieved from http://www.nytimes.com/2012/02/05/education/international-students-pay-top-dollar-at-us-colleges.html

Linda Vista Planning Group. (n.d.). *Members.* Retrieved from http://www.lindavista.org/lvpg/board.html

Loyola Center for Community Service and Justice. (n.d.). *Mission, vision, and history.* Retrieved from http://www.loyola.edu/department/ccsj/about/mission

Loyola University Maryland. (n.d.). *History and mission.* Retrieved from http://www.loyola.edu/about/history-mission

Maciag, M. (2015, February). *Gentrification in America report.* Retrieved from http://www.governing.com/gov-data/gentrification-in-cities-governing-report.html

Making College Possible. (n.d.). *College Avenue Compact.* Retrieved from https://www.collegeavenuecompact.com/Programs

Marcelli, E.A., & Pastor, M. (2015, February). *Unauthorized and uninsured: Building healthy communities in California.* Los Angeles, CA: Center for the Study of Immigrant Integration. Retrieved from http://dornsife.usc.edu/csii/unauthorized-and-uninsured

Martinez-Cosio, M., & Bussell, M. R. (2013). *Catalysts for change: Twenty-first century philanthropy and community development.* New York, NY: Routledge.

Matthews, P. H., Dorfman, P. H., & Wu, X. (2015). The impacts of undergraduate service-learning on post-graduation employment outcomes. *International Journal of Research on Service-Learning and Community Engagement, 3*(1).

McCoy, D., & Rodricks, D. J. (2015). *Critical race theory in higher education: 20 years of theoretical and research innovations* (ASHE Higher Education Report vol. 41, no. 3). Indianapolis, IN: Wiley and Sons.

McIntosh, P. (1989, July/August). White privilege: Unpacking the invisible knapsack. *Peace and Freedom,* 10–12.

Mitchell, T. (2008). Traditional vs. critical service-learning: Engaging the literature to differentiate two models. *Michigan Journal of Community Service Learning, 14(2),* 50–65.

Mitchell, T. D., Donahue, D. M., & Young-Law, C. (2012). Service learning as a pedagogy of Whiteness. *Equity and Excellence in Education, 45*(4), 612–629.

Muñoz, S. M. (2015). *Identity, social activism, and the pursuit of higher education: The journey stories of undocumented and unafraid community activists.* New York, NY: Peter Lang.

Museus, S. D., & Jayakumar, U. M. (Eds.). (2012). *Creating campus cultures: Fostering success among racially diverse student populations.* New York, NY: Routledge.

Pacific Lutheran University. (n.d.). *Parkland Education Initiative.* Retrieved from https://www.plu.edu/service/pep/

Park, J. J. (2013). *When diversity drops: Race, religion, and affirmative action in higher education.* New Brunswick, NJ: Rutgers University Press.

Patton, D. (2012, September 26). *Demographic profile of the SUYI neighborhood.* Seattle, WA: Seattle University, Center for Community Engagement.

Patton, M. Q. (2011). *Essentials of utilization focused evaluation.* Thousand Oaks, CA: Sage.

Pérez, P. A., & Ceja, M. (Eds.). (2015). *Higher education access and choice for Latino students: Critical findings and theoretical perspectives.* New York, NY: Routledge.

Perez, W. (2009). *We ARE Americans: Undocumented students pursuing the American dream.* Sterling, VA: Stylus.

Plaut J., & Hamerlinck, J. (Eds.). (2014). *Asset-based community engagement in higher education.* Minneapolis, MN: Minnesota Campus Compact.

Post, M., Ward, E., Longo, N. V., & Saltmarsh, J. (Eds.). (2016). *Next-generation engagement and the future of higher education: Publicly engaged scholars.* Sterling, VA: Stylus.

Price, R. E. (2012). *Sol Price: Retail revolutionary and social innovator.* San Diego, CA: San Diego History Center.

Ramsey, J., Bono, J., Lin, M., & Turner, N. (2016, May 18). MRC student coalition seeks radical change. *Seattle University Spectator.*

Rhoads, R. A. (1997). *Community service and higher learning: Explorations of the caring self.* Albany, NY: State University of New York Press.

Sáenz, V. B., Ponjuán, L., & López Figueroa, J. (2016). *Ensuring the success of Latino males in higher education: A national imperative.* Sterling, VA: Stylus.

San Diego State University Office of the President. (n.d.). *University history.* Retrieved from http://newscenter.sdsu.edu/ootp/history.aspx?

Santa Clara University Ignatian Center for Jesuit Education. (n.d.). *Thriving Neighbors Initiative.* Retrieved from https://www.scu.edu/ic/programs/thriving-neighbors/

Schuh, J. H., Biddix, J. P., Dean, L. A., & Kinzie, J. (2016). *Assessment methods for student affairs* (2nd ed.). San Francisco, CA: Jossey-Bass.

Seal, B. (2016, December). *How Drexel won a $30M grant for West Philadelphia schools.* Retrieved from http://drexel.edu/now/archive/2016/December/Promise-Zone-Grant/

Seattle University (n.d.). *Mission, vision, and values.* Retrieved from: https://www.seattleu.edu/about/mission/

Seattle University Place-Based Institute. (2014). *Place-based initiative institute profiles.* Seattle, WA: Author.

Seattle University Place-Based Institute. (2016). *Place-based initiative institute profiles.* Seattle, WA: Author.

Selingo, J. (2013). *College (un)bound: The future of higher education and what it means for students.* New York, NY: Houghton Mifflin Harcourt.

Silicon Valley North. (2017, May 11). *The Economist.* Retrieved from https://www.economist.com/news/business/21721950-more-ever-seattle-and-silicon-valley-are-joined-hip-how-americas-two-tech-hubs-are

Sinegal, J. (2015, October 15). *Building the case for investment: A conversation with Jim Sinegal.* San Francisco, CA: University of San Francisco, Place-Based Community Engagement Institute.

Snyder, S. (2016, May 15). College president as urban planner. *The Philadelphia Inquirer* (Special Reports). Retrieved from http://www.philly.com/philly/news/special_packages/Drexel_University_president_John_Fry_as_urban_planner.html

Stake, R. (1995). *The art of case study research.* Thousand Oaks, CA: Sage.

Statistical Atlas. (n.d.). *Population of Linda Vista.* Retrieved from http://statisticalatlas.com/neighborhood/California/San-Diego/Linda-Vista/Population

Steele, J., Salcedo, N., & Coley, J. (2010). *Service members in school: Military veterans' experiences using the Post-9/11 GI Bill and pursuing postsecondary education.* Washington DC: The American Council on Education.

Stewart, T., & Webster, N. (Eds.). (2011). *Exploring cultural dynamics & tensions within service-learning.* Charlotte, NC: Information Age.

Stoecker, R. (2016). *Liberating service learning and the rest of higher education civic engagement.* Philadelphia, PA: Temple University Press.

Stoecker R., & Tryon, E. A. (Eds.). (2009). *The unheard voices: Community organizations and service-learning.* Philadelphia, PA: Temple University Press.

Takaki, R. (1993). *A different mirror: A multicultural history of America.* New York, NY: Back Bay Books.

United by Purpose. (n.d.). *The West Phoenix turnaround story.* Retrieved from http://unitedbypurpose.com/

University of New Brunswick. (n.d.). *Promise Partnership.* Retrieved from http://www.unb.ca/saintjohn/promise/

University of Pittsburgh. (2016). *Pitt reimagines partnerships.* Retrieved from http://www.news.pitt.edu/news/pitt-reimagines-community-partnerships

University of San Diego. (n.d.). *Envisioning 2024.* Retrieved from https://www.sandiego.edu/envisioning-2024/overview/

University of San Francisco. (n.d.). *Engage San Francisco.* Retrieved from https://www.usfca.edu/mccarthy/programs/engage-san-francisco

U.S. Department of Education National Center for Education Statistics. (2016). *Digest of education statistics, 2015 (NCES 2016-014), Chapter 3.* Retrieved from https://nces.ed.gov/fastfacts/display.asp?id=76

U.S. Department of Education National Center for Education Statistics. (n.d.). *Fast facts.* Retrieved from http://www.sandiego.edu/about/facts.php

W. K. Kellogg Foundation. (2004, January). *Using logic models to bring together planning, evaluation, and action logic model development guide.* East Battle Creek, MI: Author.

Ward, H. (Ed.). (1999). *Acting locally: Concepts and models for service-learning in environmental studies.* Sterling, VA: Stylus.

Watanabe, T. (2017, July 7). UC regents approve first limit on out-of-state and international student enrollment. *Los Angeles Times.* Retrieved from http://www.latimes.com/local/education/la-essential-education-updates-southern-uc-regents-approve-first-ever-limit-on-1495123220-htmlstory.html

Welch, M. (2016). *Engaging higher education: Purpose, platforms, and programs for community engagement.* Sterling, VA: Stylus.

Yarbrough, D. B., Shulha, L. M., Hopson, R. K., & Caruthers, F. A. (2010). *The program evaluation standards: A guide for evaluators and evaluation users* (3rd ed.). Thousand Oaks, CA: Sage.

Year of the city sets the tone for 2006–2007. (2008, November 26). *Loyola Magazine.* Retrieved from http://magazine.loyola.edu/issue/date/2008/11

Yelp, R. (2015, May 1). Baltimore's demographic divide. *The Wall Street Journal.*

Yessler Community Collaborative. (n.d.). *Historic neighborhoods.* Retrieved from https://yescollab.org/

Yin, R. K. (2003). *Case study research: Design and methods* (3rd ed.). Thousand Oaks, CA: Sage.

Erica K. Yamamura is an associate professor and program liaison coordinator of the student development administration program in the College of Education at Seattle University. As a faculty member, she has utilized service-learning and community-based projects as part of her pedagogy at Carleton College, Texas State University, and Seattle University. For the last six years at Seattle University, she has engaged in project-based learning in her required student development theory course, one of the few in the country that utilizes this pedagogy in graduate education in the field of student affairs. Since 2013, Yamamura has also conducted research on promising practices arising from the Seattle University Youth Initiative.

As a graduate student in the top-ranked higher education and organizational change program at the University of California, Los Angeles (UCLA), Yamamura served as a research assistant working on a quantitative longitudinal study of service and service-learning for Alexander Astin's grant with the Atlantic Philanthropies. She also served as a teaching associate for an innovative college-access service-learning program, the Career-Based Outreach Program (CBOP) at UCLA, which provided hundreds of hours of college preparatory activities to low-income and underresourced schools in urban Los Angeles.

In addition to her teaching and scholarly activities, Yamamura has prior experience as a practitioner in the field of community engagement. She served as a site coordinator at a Title 1 majority Latina/o school in the Los Angeles Unified School District working with industries, community organizations, and local colleges to build an academic mentor program on the campus. She also served as an educational coordinator at UCLA in the Center for Community Learning where she was the liaison for the undergraduate education minor, served as an internship coordinator for educational internships, coordinated two AmeriCorps grants (Students in Service and Bonner Foundation Fellows), and maintained a number of public school partnerships as part of the UCLA in LA initiative. She received her BA in political science and Asian American studies and MA and PhD in education (higher education and organizational change) from UCLA.

Kent Koth is the founding director of the Seattle University Center for Community Engagement. In this role Koth has overseen a rapid expansion of campus-community partnerships that have received national recognition including the 2012 President's National Community Service Higher Education Award. Since 2009, he has also led the Seattle University Youth Initiative, a long-term commitment by Seattle University faculty, staff, and students from all disciplines to join with parents, the Seattle School District, the city of Seattle, foundations, and more than 30 community organizations to empower the children of Seattle to succeed in school and life.

As an adjunct faculty member in the Seattle University Interdisciplinary Liberal Studies Program, Koth has taught courses focusing on leadership and community engagement. He has also written, consulted, and presented extensively on topics of spirituality and service-learning, place-based community engagement, and the ethics of university-community partnerships.

With support from the Annie E. Casey Foundation, Koth is currently leading an effort to create a national network of faith-based universities pursuing place-based community engagement. Since 2014, Seattle University, through Koth's leadership, has organized 4 Place-Based Community Engagement Institutes for teams from 21 institutions.

Earlier in his career, Koth served as program director at the Haas Center for Public Service at Stanford University and taught several courses in the Stanford University Urban Studies Program. He also worked as executive director of youth community service in Palo Alto, California and led Willamette University's effort to create a community engagement program.

Koth's career in community engagement began when, upon finishing his undergraduate degree, he received a Samuel Huntington Public Service Fellowship to mobilize students from 10 universities and colleges in Oregon to serve and learn during their academic breaks.

Koth received his BA from Grinnell College and MA from the Pacific School of Religion in Berkeley, California. He is originally from Iowa and currently resides with his spouse and two children in Seattle, Washington.

Engaging Higher Education

Purpose, Platforms, and Programs for Community Engagement

Marshall Welch

Foreword by John Saltmarsh

"Rarely in a maturing scholarly field does a volume provide both breadth and depth of scholarship, but Marshall Welch's volume accomplishes this feat masterfully. Welch provides an overview of the community engagement field in its current state, rooted in research and scholarly analysis. From its historical origins as a movement to the evolution of community engagement as a field, this volume extends an evidence-based synthesis of how higher education systems structure and implement community engagement, as well as a 'how-to' for higher education institutions. It will serve multiple purposes for higher education administrators, faculty, community engagement center directors, and graduate students in education."—*Patrick M. Green, Founding Director, Center for Experiential Learning, Loyola University Chicago; Past Board Chair, International Association for Research on Service-Learning and Community Engagement*

22883 Quicksilver Drive
Sterling, VA 20166-2019 Subscribe to our e-mail alerts: www.Styluspub.com

The Community Engagement Professional in Higher Education

A Competency Model for an Emerging Field

Edited by Lina D. Dostilio

"[This book] advances the movement for publicly engaged scholarship giving voice to their person, place and purpose in academe with myriad inflections beyond campus borders. Couched in a conceptually rich analysis of the professions, the authors demonstrate the multidimensionality and complexity of this rising class and their critical place in the university of the twenty-first century."—*Timothy K. Eatman*, *Associate Professor, Syracuse University, Director for Research for Imagining America (IA)*.

Community-Based Research

Teaching for Community Impact

Edited by Mary Beckman and Joyce F. Long

Foreword by Timothy K. Eatman

"Skillfully organized, thoroughly researched, and clearly written, Beckman and Long have succeeded in assembling a collection of expert scholar-practitioners, each of whom provides evidence and practical advice for planning and conducting community-based research [CBR]

(Continues on preceding page)